America's Atlantic Isles

By H. Robert Morrison and Christine Eckstrom Lee • Photographed by David Alan Harvey

Prepared by the Special Publications Division • National Geographic Society, Washington, D. C.

AMERICA'S ATLANTIC ISLES

By H. Robert Morrison *and* Christine Eckstrom Lee
Photographed by David Alan Harvey

Published by
The National Geographic Society
Gilbert M. Grosvenor, *President*
Melvin M. Payne, *Chairman of the Board*
Owen R. Anderson, *Executive Vice President*
Robert L. Breeden, *Vice President, Publications and
    Educational Media*

Prepared by
The Special Publications Division
Donald J. Crump, *Editor*
Philip B. Silcott, *Associate Editor*
William L. Allen, William R. Gray, *Senior Editors*

Staff for this book
Paul D. Martin, *Managing Editor*
Thomas B. Powell III, *Picture Editor*
Suez B. Kehl, *Art Director*
Alice K. Jablonsky, Jane R. McCauley, Barbara A.
    Payne, *Senior Researchers;* Amy Goodwin, *Researcher*

Illustrations and Design
Cynthia B. Scudder, *Assistant Designer*
Richard Fletcher, D. Randy Young, *Design Assistants*
John D. Garst, Jr., Susanah B. Brown, Patricia K.
    Cantlay, Jerald N. Fishbein, Margaret Deane
    Gray, *Map Research, Design, and Production*
Jane H. Buxton, Tom Melham, H. Robert Morrison,
    Lisa Olson, Jennifer C. Urquhart, Suzanne
    Venino, *Picture Legend Writers*

Engraving, Printing, and Product Manufacture
Robert W. Messer, *Manager*
George V. White, *Production Manager*
Gregory Storer, *Production Project Manager*
Mark R. Dunlevy, Richard A. McClure, Raja D.
    Murshed, Christine A. Roberts, David V. Showers,
    Assistant Production Managers; Mary A. Bennett, Kate
    Donohue, *Production Staff Assistants*
Debra A. Antonini, Nancy F. Berry, Pamela A. Black,
    Barbara Bricks, Nettie Burke, Jane H. Buxton,
    Mary Elizabeth Davis, Claire M. Doig, Rosamund
    Garner, Victoria D. Garrett, Nancy J. Harvey,
    Joan Hurst, Suzanne J. Jacobson, Artemis S.
    Lampathakis, Virginia A. McCoy, Merrick P.
    Murdock, Cleo Petroff, Victoria I. Piscopo, Tammy
    Presley, Jane F. Ray, Carol A. Rocheleau,
    Katheryn M. Slocum, Jenny Takacs, *Staff Assistants*
Jeffrey A. Brown, *Index*

Library of Congress CIP Data: page 199.

*Fog-shrouded Bass Harbor Head Light (right), on
Maine's Mount Desert Island, flashes a warning
for fishing boats and ferries. Preceding pages:
Sandbar on Georgia's Sea Island offers solitude for
a beachcomber. Page 1: Snowy egret searches for
food in Virginia's Chincoteague National Wildlife
Refuge. Hardcover: Cape Hatteras Lighthouse
stands tall in the Outer Banks of North Carolina.*

HARDCOVER ART BY SUSAN M. JOHNSTON

Contents

Foreword

Islands off the coast of Maine—actually the summits of underwater mountains—dot the indigo waters of Penobscot Bay. Pleasure craft now anchor where 17th-century French and English warships once fought for the possession of this New World territory.

AMERICA'S ATLANTIC ISLES . . . like some vast string of pearls, these windswept lands grace our eastern shore with a beguiling beauty. The allure of the islands along the Atlantic Coast finds many forms of expression. To the north, craggy, glacier-sculpted islands of Canada and Maine lie cloaked in a mantle of evergreen. Farther south, numerous flat, sandy islands throw up a coast-hugging barrier against the sea. Off the tip of Florida, palm-studded keys sparkle in the sunshine, a subtropical paradise framed by blue skies and crystal waters.

These varied landforms support an equally diverse array of wildlife. Vast numbers of birds are found among the islands, including large flocks of waterfowl that visit here on their twice-yearly migrations. Lumbering sea turtles, such as the threatened loggerhead, continue an endless cycle as they crawl ashore to nest on island beaches. Wild ponies, alligators, tiny Key deer, and many other animals live on our eastern isles.

The waters surrounding these islands also teem with life. The richness of the Atlantic fishing grounds sparked the early settlement of many islands, creating a maritime tradition that lives on. Today the sheer beauty of the islands draws a growing number of residents, prompting a rising tide of development that in some cases has caused increasing environmental concern.

National Geographic Society staff writers H. Robert Morrison and Christine Eckstrom Lee, along with staff photographer David Alan Harvey, set out to discover the wonder of our Atlantic isles. Altogether the three spent more than a year exploring islands from Canada to Florida. They traveled to dozens of islands, from mere dots of land still in their pristine state to larger islands bustling with human activity. They also visited a small number of capes and spits, formations that share many characteristics with islands.

Although Bob, Chris, and Dave could not possibly visit all of the isles along our eastern shore—Maine alone has as many as 3,000 islands according to some counts—those islands they did visit clearly represent the abundant variety to be found. Their travels, reported in the pages that follow, reveal a world of surprising complexity, a sometimes wild and rugged world existing, paradoxically, on the doorstep of America's most densely populated region.

Gilbert M. Grosvenor

President
National Geographic Society

Afterdecks piled high with lobster pots and buoys, fishing boats on New Brunswick's Grand

the Northern Coast

By H. Robert Morrison

Manan Island churn out of Seal Cove on the way to lobstering grounds in the Bay of Fundy.

*Shaped by Ice Age glaciers and later isolated from the
mainland by rising seas, the rocky isles from New
Brunswick to New Hampshire number in the thousands.
Often remote, they boast more forests and fewer
developments than do islands farther south—despite
man's continuous presence since the early 17th century.*

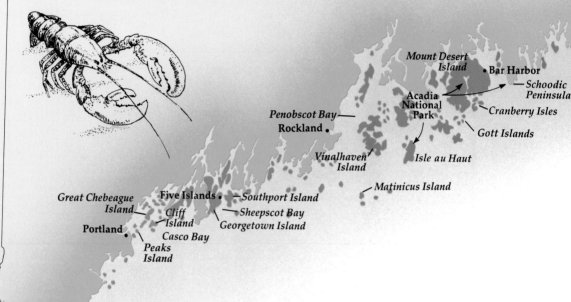

STATUTE MILES
0   25   50

0   40   80
KILOMETERS

MAINE

Mount Desert Island
• Bar Harbor
—Schoodic Peninsula
Acadia National Park
—Cranberry Isles
Gott Islands
Penobscot Bay—
Rockland •
Vinalhaven Island
Isle au Haut
Matinicus Island
Great Chebeague Island—
Five Islands •
Cliff Island
—Southport Island
Sheepscot Bay
Georgetown Island
Portland •
Casco Bay
Peaks Island

N.H.
Portsmouth•
Duck Island
Appledore Island
Isles of Shoals
Star Island

MASS.

"*I*t takes a special kind of person to be an islander." Thus
did Howard Heller, resident of tiny Peaks Island off
the southern coast of Maine, succinctly summarize
what I was to discover again and again as I explored dozens of islands along our Atlantic shore.

"I've found that islanders share certain characteristics," the 57-
year-old real estate broker explained. "They have great individuality
and a healthy respect for each other's privacy, curiously combined with a
dependence on their neighbors."

My colleague Chris Lee and I, together with staff photographer
Dave Harvey, were to learn how accurate Howard's description had
been as we visited islands large and small during many months of
travel. I began my travels in Canada's Bay of Fundy and from there
proceeded south to New Jersey. Chris, meanwhile, started on the barrier
islands off the Eastern Shore of Virginia. From there, she made her way
south to the Florida Keys.

At the very outset of my travels, the interdependence of islanders
described by Howard Heller sprang vividly to life. As I sat in the neat
living room of Vernon Bagley's home on Grand Manan Island, I could
sense the strong bonds that often develop among those who live on lands
surrounded by the sea. A muscular man who looks younger than his 65
years, Vernon Bagley serves as game warden on Grand Manan, a 55-
square-mile island about 17 miles off the coast of New Brunswick.

Like the other craggy islands scattered along the northern coast,
Grand Manan was sculpted by Ice Age glaciers that edged southward
from the Arctic. The glaciers gouged out areas of the soft sedimentary
rock found in this region, leaving behind a series of coastal mountains

MAP ART BY SUSANAH B. BROWN

Bay of Fundy

Grand Manan Island

Machias Seal Island

Atlantic Ocean

made of harder volcanic material. When the last glacier receded some 15,000 years ago, these mountains rose higher as the tremendous weight of the ice was removed.

At the same time, the level of the sea rose, fed by waters released from the melting ice. The rising waters flooded the coastal lowlands, isolating the mountaintops and forming the thousands of rocky islands that today fringe the coast as far south as New Hampshire.

Leaning back in his chair, Vernon Bagley recalled for me a bleak winter night of 18 years ago on Grand Manan. I could almost feel the chill wind blow as he spoke. "A phone call shortly after midnight woke me up," Vernon told me. " 'Someone's over the cliff at Southwest Head,' the operator said. It was February 1963, and a gale was beating snow across the whole island.

" 'Well, I'd best get crackin',' I said to my wife.

"When I got to the lighthouse at Southwest Head, I discovered that two fishermen, brothers, had been flung aground at the base of the 200-foot cliff after their boat's engine had failed in the storm. They had managed to pull themselves above the surf. One of them had somehow scaled the cliff and, half dead, had alerted the lighthouse keeper.

"Nobody wanted to go down the cliff after a man who might by then be a corpse. But I kept thinking, 'What if it was my own brother down there?' and I volunteered to try. I tied a rope around my waist and went over the edge while the men at the top anchored the other end. I had gone only a few yards down a ridge when loose rock gave way and I lost my footing. The men hauled me up. It seemed hopeless.

"But something inside me made me try again. This time I left the ridge and climbed down kind of sideways. When I was about 150 feet down, I heard a low voice. I shined my flashlight over to the left and saw the other victim. 'Help me,' he called. I inched my way over to him. When I reached the fisherman, I found that he was frozen from the waist down and couldn't move his legs. My wife had packed an extra pair of mittens in my pocket, and I managed to get them onto his hands. Then I tied the rope around both of our waists and began the climb back up.

"We hadn't gone far when he passed out. I thought to myself, 'If he is as scared as I am, he's better off unconscious.' The climb seemed like it was three nights long. Several times I lost my grip, and the wind was so strong it actually blew me against the cliff and kept me from falling.

"About ten yards from the top I gave out," Vernon continued. "I wedged the fisherman behind a boulder where I knew he'd be safe, and the men pulled me in. The assistant lighthouse keeper went down on another rope and got him. We rushed the men to the hospital, and they both pulled through. As for me, I thought I'd never thaw out," he concluded. "My wife said I looked like I was 90 years old when I got home!"

For his bravery, Vernon Bagley was awarded a Silver Medal for Heroism by the Carnegie Hero Fund Commission, an organization established in 1904 by industrialist Andrew Carnegie to recognize acts of heroism in the United States and Canada.

"I wasn't trying to be a hero," he said. "I just thought about the man down there, and I knew if he was my brother I'd go. And then I thought, 'We're all brothers.' And I went."

After hearing Vernon Bagley's story about the shipwrecked fishermen, I was relieved that fair weather was forecast, for I was scheduled to spend the following day aboard a lobster boat off Grand Manan. I was

eager to see the local lobstermen in action. The rich offshore fishing grounds of Grand Manan attracted Europeans as early as the 17th century, and today fishing is still a mainstay of the economy. Modern lobstermen must be willing to risk a five-figure investment in a boat and traps that storms can devastate, to face the ever-present dangers of the sea, and to perform backbreaking labor in all kinds of weather.

It was 5 a.m. when I arrived at the pier the lobster boat was to leave from, in the small fishing settlement of Ingalls Head. A few herring gulls seemed to be the only other creatures awake at this early hour. Then a pickup truck swung down the pier, its headlights piercing the thick fog.

J. Wayne Ingalls and Evan Johnson, the fishermen who had invited me aboard for a day's work, climbed down and began transferring gear to Wayne's boat, the *Jayne & Jill*—"the first fiberglass lobster boat on Grand Manan," Wayne proudly told me. Most of the local boats are made of wood, just as they have been built here for nearly 200 years. The two stocky young men worked quickly, the thick muscles of their arms and shoulders bulging with their efforts. Half an hour later as we headed eastward, I asked if they always started out at this hour.

"Well, it depends on the tide," Evan said. "But we like to get the work done early."

"Yes," Wayne agreed, pushing back the Baltimore Orioles baseball cap he wore. "By nine o'clock in the morning, the day's almost gone."

Both men donned rubberized overalls when we approached the location of the traps, near the shipping channel in the Bay of Fundy

Millions of discarded scallop shells litter a deserted beach on Grand Manan, a testament to the ocean's bounty—and to the success of local fishermen. Fishing and lobstering dominate the economy of the island, which lies six miles off the easternmost point of Maine. In addition to herring and shellfish, residents harvest pearl essence, a substance derived from fish scales and used in the manufacture of costume jewelry, shirt buttons, lip gloss, and fire-extinguisher foam.

about 14 miles from the Nova Scotia shore. Evan removed the cover from a barrel behind the pilothouse. As a pungent odor scented the air, he began filling the plastic bait cups with salted herring.

Two hours after leaving Ingalls Head, which is named for Wayne Ingalls's family, we spotted the float on the first of Wayne's four lines of traps. Pulling it in with a boat hook, Wayne passed the line around a large bronze pulley and flipped a lever beside him. Glistening droplets sprayed from the line as the spinning pulley rapidly hauled it in.

I had seen countless round-topped wooden lobster traps stacked to dry all about the island, but when the first of Wayne's traps broke the surface I saw that it was not like them. It was made of heavy plastic-coated steel netting. Shaped like a rectangular box, it was much larger than the wooden traps. Wayne explained that Canada has a minimum legal size of lobster, but no maximum—unlike Maine, which sets upper and lower limits on the size of a legal lobster. "The big ones we catch out here," he commented, "couldn't even get into those wooden traps."

Wayne and Evan worked smoothly together. As each of the 14 traps was raised they would rest it on the gunwale, pry back the elastic bands that secured the door on the top of the trap, then flip the door open. After removing the lobsters inside, they untied the bait cup, dumped its contents overboard, and added fresh bait.

Evan then coiled the line on top of the trap and carried it to the stern. When all the traps had been emptied and stacked at the stern, Wayne gunned the engine as Evan tossed the (Continued on page 18)

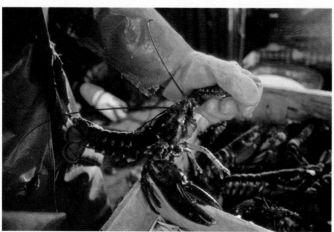

F lecks of sea salt freckle the face of Peter Wilcox, 26-year-old lobsterman from Grand Manan (above). Beginning each November, when the season opens, Wilcox and islanders such as Ronald Brown (opposite, top) challenge giant tides and wintry seas in pursuit of lobsters (left). Pots must be hauled up one at a time (opposite), emptied of their

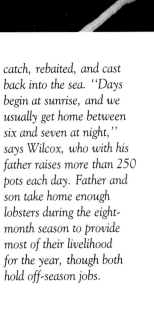

catch, rebaited, and cast
back into the sea. "Days
begin at sunrise, and we
usually get home between
six and seven at night,"
says Wilcox, who with his
father raises more than 250
pots each day. Father and
son take home enough
lobsters during the eight-
month season to provide
most of their livelihood
for the year, though both
hold off-season jobs.

Adult Atlantic puffin clutches a beakful of herring on Machias Seal Island, off Grand Manan. Spending most of the year at sea, these pigeon-size birds return every April to the islands and coastal areas where they hatched. There they nest in large seaside colonies. Female puffins usually lay a single egg in a crevice or a burrow dug as deep as six feet. To dig a burrow, the birds use their powerful beaks to loosen the dirt, then shovel out the debris with their webbed feet. Pairs share parental duties, feeding fish to their young for about six weeks. After that the young birds can survive on their own.

first trap overboard. The line payed out rapidly, and each trap in turn automatically slid up a ramp and flew overboard.

The catch from the first line of traps had been disappointing. There were fewer than half a dozen lobsters, and only one or two of them weighed more than a couple of pounds or so. As Wayne and Evan joked about their bait being no more than expensive fish food, I began to wonder if I had brought bad luck aboard with me. But the second line produced a better catch. A number of traps held two or three lobsters each, and one of them was a monster—15 or 16 pounds, Evan guessed.

After a break for lunch, while we waited for the tide to crest and slacken, we hauled in and reset the last two of Wayne's lines. These, too, produced good catches. We headed for home about five in the afternoon with more than 350 pounds of lobsters—about right for an average day's work, Wayne and Evan agreed.

*E*arly in my travels, I was to discover the importance of lobstering throughout the northern coastal islands. I also found that lobster fishing in this region has changed considerably over the years. A man who remembers how it was long ago is Charlie Gott. Charlie is a short, lively man with an unruly shock of white hair and powerfully built arms and shoulders. His light blue eyes sparkle in his weather-beaten face, and he has a quick sense of humor.

"I began lobstering when I was 7 years old," he told my wife, Meredith, and me in the snug parlor of his home on Mount Desert Island, off the central coast of Maine. "That was in 1904 on Great Gott Island, which was named for my family. A neighbor gave me 13 old traps and I worked them from a rowboat. I got 15 cents apiece for those lobsters."

His family, he told us, had settled both the Gott Islands—two spots of rock just south of Mount Desert. They settled Great Gott when George Washington was President. "I grew up on Great Gott, but even then people were leaving the island," Charlie recalled. "When my father attended the island school he had fifty or sixty classmates. When I went there, enrollment had dropped to about eighteen or twenty.

"When I got old enough, I helped my father. He owned a Friendship sloop, a good boat that was easy to handle and would stand most any weather. Why, you could blow the canvas right off it," Charlie said. "Life on Great Gott was good. Everybody helped each other. It was like one big family. My father and all of my uncles went lobstering—there was no other way to make a living. And there were plenty of lobsters then. Sometimes we'd haul the traps twice a day.

"But my family decided to leave Gott Island," Charlie continued. "It just became too isolated there. The thing I remember most about why we left is that we thought how nice it would be to go for a drive sometimes, like on Sunday afternoons. But there were no cars and no roads on Gott Island. So we moved to Mount Desert Island, which already had cars and roads.

"I went lobstering every year from 1904 until 1979," Charlie concluded. "I never got rich, of course. We always managed to get by, but it usually took all we could make."

While lobstering remains important to the economy of Mount Desert, tourism is now the island's chief industry. Thousands of visitors are drawn each year to Acadia National Park, much of which is located on the 108-square-mile island. On a bright afternoon in early summer,

Herring boats off Grand Manan corral a watery catch. The boats work near a large fish trap known as a weir. Herring swim close to shore at night to feed or to escape predators. They turn at the net strung from the island to the kidney-shaped weir. After the fish enter the weir's mouth, workers aboard the seine boat, at right, encircle them with a purse seine and haul it to the surface. Next, the pumper boat, in the middle, transfers the herring to the third boat, at left, which shuttles the catch to port. There workers freeze the fish, can them, or cure them with smoke.

Meredith and I hiked to the top of St. Sauveur Mountain within the park. After an easy climb along a tree-shaded trail, we rested for a short time at the summit and then continued southeastward to Flying Mountain, overlooking the entrance to Somes Sound.

The air was clear and crisp, and the scenery was breathtaking. Spread out in a panorama below us were the island ports of Northeast Harbor and Southwest Harbor. White-sailed yachts cut through the sparkling sea beyond. Farther to the southeast lay Great and Little Cranberry Islands, named for the cranberry bog found on the larger isle.

To the northeast, evergreen-clad mountains rose from the sun-dappled waters of narrow Somes Sound, the only true fjord on the eastern coast of the United States. After a steep descent to Somes Sound, we enjoyed a stroll over an old gravel road along Man of War Brook. I had learned earlier how this stream received its name. Where it tumbles into Somes Sound, 18th-century British warships once anchored within a few yards of shore. While the ships were anchored there, sailors could easily replenish their supplies of fresh water from the stream.

The gravel road reminded me of another facet of Mount Desert's history. During the late 1800s, the island was discovered as a summer resort by the rich. Among those who summered here was the financier John D. Rockefeller, Jr. To provide access to many of Mount Desert's beauty spots, he built a network of graded gravel carriage roads. Today

some forty miles of these broad, smooth roads remain in Acadia National Park, attracting bicyclists and strollers of all ages.

Early one summer morning, Meredith and I drove up the winding road that leads to the 1,530-foot-high summit of Mount Desert's Cadillac Mountain, the highest coastal mountain on the U. S. Atlantic shore. The beams of our headlights reflected back from patches of fog in the predawn blackness.

It was the morning of the Fourth of July. Because for much of the year Cadillac Mountain is the first place the sun strikes in the United States, we planned to begin our holiday by observing the sunrise there. And we looked forward to joining a group of people in one of the most unusual Independence Day celebrations we had heard of.

A few minutes after we pulled into the parking lot at the summit, the area began stirring with activity. Continuing a 12-year tradition, Mount Desert's square dance club—the Acadian Bells and Buoys—was preparing for its Independence Day dance on the mountaintop. Lively music soon sounded from a portable public-address system set up at the back of a pickup truck. With caller Phil Junkins at the microphone, and with the asphalt of the parking lot as the dance floor, forty couples began swinging in time to the music.

Then at the moment of sunrise, a few minutes before 5 a.m., the

Ghostly forest of net and pilings surrounds fishermen tending a Grand Manan herring weir. Anchored in waters as deep as 65 feet, the wood poles and custom-made netting demand constant attention. Unlike trawlers, fixed weirs can neither run from bad weather nor follow the schools of herring, but they offer fishermen other advantages. They remain close to port for easy access, and they can serve as holding pens for catches awaiting processing.

music stopped. We all faced the flagpole and joined in the national anthem as Old Glory rose flapping in the breeze. As we sang, I glanced at the people around me. From teen-agers to retired couples, they seemed to me a cross section of Americans, and I could think of no better way to start the Fourth of July.

Our celebration that day continued with a boat trip to Islesford, a community on Little Cranberry Island, just south of Mount Desert. I had visited there earlier on a U. S. Park Service cruise conducted by naturalist Bill Townsend.

"Although many people think of the Pilgrims of Plymouth, Massachusetts, as the first settlers on the New England coast," Bill had told us, "several fishing villages were established earlier farther north. The Indian Samoset, for example, was able to greet the Pilgrims in English when they arrived. He had learned to speak English from fishermen living along the coast of what is now the state of Maine.

"Many early settlements were located on the smaller islands offshore," Bill had added. "They were often settled before the mainland or the larger islands because they were closer to the good fishing grounds. When the first permanent settler on Mount Desert, Abraham Somes, brought his family to the island in 1762, some of the small islands nearby already had people living on them." (Continued on page 29)

ewly married Ernest Dougherty (above) spins his bride, Lil, atop 1,530-foot Cadillac Mountain during a predawn Fourth of July square dance on Mount Desert Island. When the sun poked above the horizon, the dancers paused for a flag-raising ceremony and the playing of the "Star-Spangled Banner." Other festivities help Maine islanders celebrate the nation's birthday with more than parades and fireworks. Boiled lobsters (opposite, top) invite mouth-watering appraisals at a cookout on Little Cranberry Island. In Mount Desert's coastal resort town of Bar Harbor, a community band gives an evening concert on the village green (right).

"*I thought 75 years of lobstering—alone mostly—was about enough. So I retired,*" *recalls 84-year-old Charlie Gott (below), who now spends more time with his wife, Hazel, in their Mount Desert home. Gott considers Maine's largest island "just about the best around. We've got forests, fields, mountains, fresh water, salt water, fish of all kinds, animals, just about anything you could want." At right, hardworking lobster boats rest on their moorings in one of the island's fog-draped harbors. Most people now associate Mount Desert less with lobstermen than with sleek yachts, artists' colonies, and lavish summer homes. Morgans and Rockefellers, Astors and Vanderbilts*

summered here at the turn of the century, when Bar Harbor rivaled Newport, Rhode Island, as the prime vacation spot for America's wealthy. Seasonal residents today equal in number the island's 9,200 year-round dwellers.

Wispy clouds and dark stands of conifers shroud islands in three-mile-wide Sheepscot Bay.

Maine's islands number as high as 3,000, depending on the observer's definition of an island.

Breakers claw the rock-strewn coast of Mount Desert, named in 1604 by the French explorer Samuel de Champlain for its craggy, treeless peaks. The wild grandeur of Mount Desert awed John D. Rockefeller, Jr., who along with other prominent summer residents began setting aside private preserves in the early 1900s. These lands now belong to 34,450-acre Acadia National Park, first national park established east of the Mississippi. Acadia also encompasses land on Schoodic Peninsula and much of Isle au Haut.

Arriving at Islesford shortly after noon, Meredith and I joined a group of year-round residents and summer people in the community's Fourth of July picnic. Tables set up in a field at the edge of the harbor held crisp green salad and home-baked cupcakes, cookies, and biscuits. There were bright-red lobsters, fresh from great pots of boiling seawater, and crisp pieces of chicken barbecued over charcoal fires.

While waiting for a potful of lobsters to cook, I introduced myself to Maggie Ritteman, president of the Islesford Neighborhood House Association. "We're hoping to raise enough money here today," she told me, "to replace some of the shingles on our neighborhood house, which serves the island as a community center and library.

"We hold poetry readings, community sings, suppers, and occasional concerts there. Once in a while we'll have square dancing or contra dancing. About 300 to 350 people live in Islesford in the summer, but in winter the island's population drops to about a hundred. We try to continue programs through the winter," she said. "You have to keep pretty busy here, or you can get cabin fever."

I was to learn more about the isolation that Mrs. Ritteman alluded to the following February when I visited the small island of Matinicus, some 16 miles off Maine's central coast. With a winter population of about fifty, Matinicus has only twice-a-week scheduled boat service to connect it to the mainland. From the Mount Desert port of Northeast Harbor, I left for Matinicus aboard the 65-foot ship *Sunbeam,* a private vessel owned by the Maine Sea Coast Missionary Society.

As the ship pitched and rolled in six-foot seas, I chatted with my host, Minister-in-Charge Stanley B. Haskell. Stan, as he prefers to be called, explained the mission of his organization. "Since 1905," he told me, "the Maine Sea Coast Missionary Society has served the people of the islands and coastal communities of eastern Maine. During our monthly visits to isolated islands such as Matinicus, we provide religious and social services for villages too small to support a full-time minister."

Arriving on Matinicus after our four-hour boat trip, I visited the island's schoolhouse, where 32-year-old Sari Ryder was teaching elementary classes for a total of three pupils. Sari told me what it is like to live on the island, where life is so different from the life she had known in her mainland home of Rockport.

"I was prepared for the isolation," she said with a smile. "I brought a lot of books I had never found time to read, and I also brought some handicraft projects—several rugs to hook, for example. At first I wanted to visit the mainland every weekend. But now, every six weeks is often enough. And after a day or so, I'm glad to get back to Matinicus."

After ending our stay on Mount Desert, Meredith and I headed southwest to visit Vinalhaven, one of the largest islands in Penobscot Bay. Vinalhaven is seven and a half miles long and five miles wide. However, so many coves and inlets lace its coastline that no point on the island is more than a mile from salt water.

Vinalhaven today relies primarily on fishing and lobstering for its livelihood, though in earlier days it was known for the granite quarried there. Some of the island's abandoned granite quarries now serve a new purpose: Filled with clear spring water, they make ideal swimming holes. Indeed, Vinalhaven's quarrying past remains visible throughout the island. Meredith and I walked a short distance up a shady unpaved road to Isle au Haut Mountain, where rough-hewn stone blocks gave us vantage points for island-spangled Hurricane Sound. Later we hiked to the top of Tiptoe Mountain, an island park near Browns Head Light. Vistas of sparkling water dotted with green islands spread before us, and we concluded that the trip to Vinalhaven was worthwhile just for the sweeping views it affords of Penobscot Bay.

Southwest of Vinalhaven lies Casco Bay, once thought to hold as many islands as there are days in the year. Accordingly, this group became known as the Calendar Islands. "Of course, there aren't really 365 islands out there," my friend Howard Heller told me over lunch near his office in the mainland city of Portland. "How many there are depends on your definition of an island," Howard said. "Some authorities have counted 220 or more of them."

I asked Howard to explain something of what life has been like for him on Peaks Island, where he now lives. "I moved to Peaks in 1976," he said, "because I had romantic ideas about living on an island. Since then, I've learned that there are problems, too.

"For example, I need two automobiles—one on the island and one that remains on the mainland. It's just too expensive to ferry a car back and forth every day. And if my wife and I want to go to a concert or a play in town, we sometimes have to spend the night here, because the

last ferry may already have left before it's over. But there are compensations, too. If I miss the 5:30 evening ferry, I have to wait up to two and a half hours for the next one. I'm seldom tempted to spend an extra hour at the office! The twenty-minute boat trip after a day's work has an effect that's hard to describe. You have time to relax and think. And the sunsets," he smiled, "are an extra bonus."

I learned more about the island life that Howard spoke of from

Ansel B. Sterling, a noted artist and educator who was born on Peaks Island. Ansel, whose family has lived on Peaks since the early 1800s, is the author of *An Island Speaks*, a history of his birthplace. He and his wife, Gladys, welcomed me to their home, "Easterling."

"Peaks's early years were those of a tiny fishing community," Ansel told me. "As late as 1800, there were only four houses on the island. But as Portland grew into a city, Peaks became a popular spot for picnics. An open-air bowling alley was established in the 1850s, and the island gradually began to cater to the summer trade. With the establishment in the 1880s of the Greenwood Garden Theater—one of America's first summer theaters—followed by an amusement park and resort hotels built during the same decade, Peaks became a lively summer resort.

"I can remember working at the Oceanic House hotel as a young man," Ansel recalled. "I washed dishes and waited tables. My most vivid memory is of a summer evening when I tripped and fell while I was carrying a huge tray of sherbet dishes to the refrigerator for chilling. Glasses flew everywhere. I was so embarrassed I took to my heels and didn't stop running until I was home!

"Although I had to leave to pursue my career as a teacher," he said, "I always missed the island. I returned for vacations whenever I could. And when I retired in the late 1960s, I moved here.

"I'm at home here," he concluded. "I belong to this island."

When I arrived on Great Chebeague, one of the largest of the islands in Casco Bay, my taxi driver, Mrs. Fran Calder, gave me a running commentary on the island and its history. As we drove along, she pointed out the houses built by the ship captains whose "stone sloops" carried Maine granite to ports along the East Coast. Although some of the vessels that sailed from Chebeague carried ballast stones to Maine shipyards as early as the late 1700s, the stone sloops reached their heyday after the Civil War. The sloops carried stone for breakwaters, for lighthouses, for street paving, and for building such edifices as the Washington Monument, in Washington, D. C.

Chebeague, like Peaks, shared in the tourist industry. In the late 1800s, islanders took in boarders for the summer. Soon vacationers began buying waterfront property and building cottages. Hotels catered to thousands of other visitors. Around the turn of the century, Postmaster Henry Bowen saw an opportunity and made the most of it. To spread Chebeague's name, and thereby attract more visitors, Bowen placed mailboxes conveniently about the island and had picture postcards printed by the thousand. Soon the little island post office could report an astonishing amount of outgoing mail as visitors wrote home to friends and family describing the charm of Chebeague.

In contrast to Chebeague, nearby Cliff Island never became a tourist center. Its population of some 450 during the summer drops to about 70 in the fall. One resident who lives here all year, Miss Johanna von Tiling, invited Meredith and me to lunch when we visited Cliff Island. An erect woman with gray hair and a ready smile, Johanna lives in the home her parents bought as a summer residence in 1923.

Her father, a physician, scholar, and music lover, had first brought his wife and daughter on a Cliff Island vacation nine years earlier, and the family had returned many summers after that. "My parents loved Cliff Island," Johanna told us, "and in 1949, after the death of my

Eyes riveted on his next handhold, Outward Bound student Bob Hicks scales a rocky cliff face on Mount Desert, in Acadia National Park. Each year, Outward Bound's school-without-walls on Penobscot Bay offers courses stressing skills such as seamanship, cross-country skiing, rock-climbing, and rappelling—as well as self-reliance and teamwork.

mother several years earlier, my father and I moved here permanently. I've been living here ever since."

Johanna's home nearly overflows with mementos of her travels, her accomplishments as a singer, and her worldwide circle of friends. As the three of us ate lunch on her cool, tree-shaded front porch, she reminisced about some of the changes she has seen on Cliff Island. "The two biggest changes were the coming of electricity in 1938 and telephones in 1963," she said matter-of-factly. "They've made life easier here. But nothing has changed the peaceful atmosphere."

After lunch Johanna chauffeured us around the island's roads—all of them unpaved—making stops at the post office and the single general store on the island. Johanna had mentioned that the people who owned the store were newcomers to the community. As we waited in the small one-room building for Johanna to make her purchases, I asked Anita Buttrick how she and her husband happened to become the storekeepers here on Cliff Island.

"Two years ago we were living in Massachusetts," she explained. "My husband, Bob, was becoming tired of the travel required in his job. One summer afternoon Bob was waiting in line at an airline counter when a man rudely pushed in front of him. The man was in such a rush that he forgot his newspaper. My husband picked it up and while reading it on the airplane noticed an ad for this store. Within two weeks we had visited the store and agreed to buy it!

"It was a drastic change from life in Massachusetts, and it took some getting used to," Mrs. Buttrick admitted. "But my husband and I love Cliff Island, and we've never regretted coming here."

"A stern and lovely scene," author Nathaniel Hawthorne wrote in 1852 of the Isles of Shoals, the farthest south of Maine's islands and the only coastal islands of New Hampshire. Even today his description remains accurate, as Meredith and I discovered when we visited there in late summer. Lying about ten miles offshore from Portsmouth, New Hampshire, this group of nine rocky islets straddles the border between Maine and New Hampshire. In the early 17th century, two wealthy Englishmen were granted title to the Isles of Shoals. In 1635 the men drew a boundary that divided the islands between them. To this day, the boundary remains unchanged.

Accompanying us to the islands was Peter Randall, an author and photographer who has written and lectured extensively on the Isles of Shoals. Peter summed up the history of the islands during the hour-long ferry ride from Portsmouth. He explained that since the 1600s the abundance of the fish in the nearby waters, coupled with the Shoalers' superior method of preserving their catch, had supported the islanders. In 1848 tourism began to become a factor here. In that year, former lighthouse keeper Thomas Laighton built a resort hotel on Appledore Island. The Appledore Hotel soon became a fashionable gathering place, attracting especially writers and artists.

In the 1870s a second resort hotel was built in the Isles of Shoals. This hotel, the Oceanic, was on Star Island across the harbor from Appledore. The Laighton family soon purchased the Oceanic Hotel. At the turn of the century, a prominent member of the Unitarian Church, Thomas Elliott, began a series of religious conferences at the Oceanic. Since World War I, the Star Island Corporation has

Near-empty schoolhouse on remote Matinicus Island claims a winter student population of only three— for preschool through eighth grade. Teacher Sari Ryder helps her trio of students make Valentine's Day mobiles from plastic milk jugs and construction paper. English fishermen settled this island near Penobscot Bay in the 17th century. Today most residents fish for a living.

purchased Star, Duck Island, and most of Appledore Island. Today the religious conferences begun by Thomas Elliott continue on Star Island, booked solid every summer.

On the broad front porch of the Oceanic Hotel, I talked with Frederick T. McGill, Jr., historian for the Star Island Corporation. McGill told me that each year, when the conference season ends, the island's population drops from some 300 to 2—the couple that serves as caretakers of Star. He also told me something of what this island means to him.

"More than anything else," he said, "Star Island represents stability and continuity—a kind of anchor in my life. I came here first in 1922, and I've served on the staff for thirty years. Here I met my wife in 1925. Our children worked here, helping in the hotel. I have made lasting friendships on the island, ones renewed every summer." McGill then expressed an attitude I was to encounter more than once during my travels. "Looking back at the mainland from here at sea," he said softly, "gives us a perspective on our everyday lives ashore."

The following afternoon, amid a flurry of farewells, Meredith and I caught the ferry that would carry us from these rockbound isles. With Canada and Maine at our stern, my thoughts turned to the islands that lay ahead of us—to Nantucket and the isles to the south.

*T*idal pool on Maine's Southport Island (opposite, top) holds remarkably varied shore life. Visible at low tide, the area surrounding the pool spans four major tidal zones. Life forms found here include northern starfish (left), which live in the lowest tidal zone, named "chondrus" for the Irish moss, Chondrus crispus, *that proliferates there. Higher up lies the rockweed zone, home of common periwinkles and the fingerlike seaweed called knotted wrack (below). Next comes the barnacle zone, followed by the black, or high intertidal, zone, which embraces surface pools that sometimes contain organisms from lower zones. For example, one strand of knotted wrack (opposite, bottom) supports both a periwinkle from the rockweed zone and five marine springtails, associated with the high intertidal zone.*

Pleasure craft cluster off the village of Five Islands, along the central coast of Maine. The

village name stems from five closely grouped isles: Georgetown, Malden, Crow, Mink, and Hen. 37

*S*now blankets a pier on Peaks Island (left),
at the harbor entrance of Portland,
Maine. Legally part of the city, Peaks
has become both a summer resort and a year-
round island suburb. The most densely populated
island in Casco Bay, Peaks lies close enough to
Portland for residents to hold city jobs, yet far
enough away for them to follow small-town life-
styles. A ferry to and from downtown serves the
island as both school bus and commuter train
(below). High-school student Richard Elliott
(opposite, bottom) returns to Peaks after a day on
the mainland. Once considered Maine's answer
to Coney Island, Peaks developed into a seasonal
entertainment center in the second half of the
19th century, when open-air bowling, skating,
hot-air balloon shows, musicals, and vaudeville
acts lured summer crowds from the mainland.

Tawny grasses cloak fields in Chilmark, on Martha's Vineyard, where a summer resident stops to pet

England Neighbors
By H. Robert Morrison

a friendly horse. Famed for its nautical past, Martha's Vineyard also has a long history of farming.

A veil of fog hung over the harbor as I strolled along the waterfront of Nantucket town early one June morning. The cedar shingles of buildings lining Old North Wharf, weathered to a gray several shades deeper than the color of the fog, were reflected in the still water. Only the haunting cry of a herring gull broke the silence. At this peaceful moment, Nantucket's nickname, "The Little Gray Lady," seemed particularly appropriate.

I knew, however, that a shrieking horn would soon announce the arrival of the day's first ferry from the mainland. A crowd of visitors would disembark, and automobiles would begin filling the streets of this historic seaport. Each year, Nantucket plays host to hundreds of thousands of tourists. Many of these visitors are drawn to the island by its rich nautical heritage. Once the home of New England's largest whaling fleet, Nantucket today retains much of the flavor of its seafaring past.

As I strolled by the tidy shops that line lower Main Street in Nantucket town, I was struck by the efforts modern-day Nantucketers are making to keep alive the island's traditions. One way they are doing this is by perpetuating traditional island crafts. I saw one such craft being practiced when I visited the shop of Nancy Chase, who along with her partner Norma Minstrell fashions and sells scrimshaw—the decoratively carved pieces of ivory long associated with Nantucket's whaling history. I had read previously how the craft of scrimshaw developed. Before the first Europeans settled on Nantucket in 1659, the Indians living here had put out to sea in small boats to fish. The Indians occasionally captured whales near the island. After the Europeans arrived, whaling gradually became an important business.

By the mid-1700s, whale oil was in great demand as a fuel. Oil from the sperm whale was especially prized for its clear, smokeless flame. The price of whale oil rose. Fortunes could be made, and Nantucketers seized the opportunity. They outfitted ships to pursue their prey, and as the numbers of nearby whales declined, their voyages became longer. Trips around Cape Horn to the Pacific often lasted two years or more. To fill their spare time, many sailors carved whale ivory or bone into articles such as piecrust crimpers, jewelry, and corset stays. Men with artistic ability etched scenes, often of their encounters with whales, onto whale teeth or slabs cut from them. Both the craft and the products became known as scrimshaw. The artisans came to be called scrimshanders.

"Ivory is an ideal material for an artist," Nancy Chase told me. "It's soft enough to be carved, it can be polished to a high luster, and it is very durable. Today ivory is expensive. No whale ivory can be imported into the United States because it comes from endangered animals. We do some work in sperm whale ivory bought before the U. S. ban on commercial importation went into effect in 1970. We can also get ivory from the tusks of African elephants and prehistoric mammoths."

As I talked with Nancy, her sister Phyllis Burchell, and other artists in the shop, I asked how one would describe a Nantucketer. It was Esther Johnson who spoke up. "Nantucketers," she stated, "are versatile and independent—especially the women of the island. After all, for years Nantucket women maintained households, raised families, took care of farms, and looked after businesses while their men went to sea. They had to be independent and versatile. And they still are."

The men and women of Nantucket were willing to endure the loneliness brought on by prolonged voyages because whaling provided a good

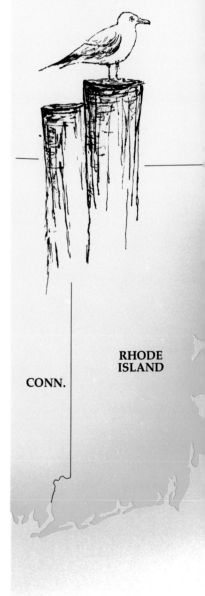

Islands off Cape Cod signal a change from the rocky isles to the north. Martha's Vineyard, four miles from the Cape, and Nantucket, twenty-four miles offshore, mark the southern limit of the last Ice Age glacier that covered New England. As the glacier receded, it left behind its burden of sand, clay, and gravel. The buildup of this debris formed the low, rolling islands in this area.

RHODE
ISLAND

CONN.

MAP ART BY SUZANNE BURTON

living. Captain, officers, and crew all received a share in the profits of the voyage. For example, in the early 19th century a cabin boy, the lowest paid member of the crew, sailed from Nantucket aboard the whaler *Lion.* He received $300 as his share of the profits—paid in cash in one lump sum after the voyage. That was as much as a day laborer could earn in a year, and the cabin boy received food and lodging aboard ship. But the bulk of the money went to the men who owned the ships. From that same voyage of the *Lion,* the shipowners' profit was $24,000—more than enough to buy and equip another ship.

The profits from whaling voyages enabled some Nantucketers to build elaborate houses. An example is the Hadwen House-Satler Memorial, a whale oil merchant's Greek-Revival mansion located on Main Street in Nantucket town. This white clapboard mansion, with its imposing two-story columns, is now maintained by the Nantucket Historical Association. The interior features many touches that indicate the wealth of the builder, such as solid silver doorknobs and shutter knobs.

Across the street from the Hadwen House-Satler Memorial stand the "Three Bricks"—three identical mansions built by shipowner Joseph Starbuck for his sons in the late 1830s. By that time, Nantucket had become the third richest community in Massachusetts, surpassed only by Boston and Salem. But the prosperity waned as Nantucket was beset with difficulties, including a fire in 1846 that destroyed much of the town. By the late 1850s decline had begun to set in, a decline aggravated by the introduction of kerosene as a substitute for whale oil. A depression that lasted nearly two decades struck Nantucket and was relieved only by the beginning of the tourist industry in the 1870s. During those lean years, there was no incentive to replace the older structures on the island. As a result, Nantucket's historical district today contains nearly 600 homes built between the late 17th and mid-19th centuries.

O ne source of income during the hard times was the manning of the lightships anchored offshore to warn of the dangerous Nantucket shoals. As a hobby, the lightships' crews often wove sturdy round or oval baskets to be used in Nantucket homes. Today the craft has been revived, and the distinctive baskets, now frequently used as purses, are recognized both on and off the island. To see how they are made, I visited The Basket Case, the workshop of Michael J. Kane.

"I've been making lightship baskets for 11 of my 24 years," Michael told me. "My grandparents taught me the craft when I was a boy."

Michael begins each basket with a framework of hand-shaped oak staves set into a base of birch or other fine wood and steamed into shape. The next step is the weaving. Michael showed me how he pulls the damp rattan taut, forming a weave so tight the basket feels almost as stiff as if it had been carved from solid wood. The top and bottom of the basket are finished with rattan-bound rims and the lid joined by leather hinges. The handle is made of hand-carved oak. Michael may add a scrimshaw decoration on the lid. For good luck, a bright new penny dated with the year he made the basket is set into the bottom inside.

Another craft item I learned about was the distinctive sign known as the quarter board. In the days of sail, these fancily carved boards displayed a ship's name on her quarters, the sides of the vessel near the stern. Today similar boards often hang above the doors of homes. Stores and other businesses use them as signboards. *(Continued on page 58)*

Morning fog rolls over Old North Wharf, on Nantucket. During the 19th-century commercial

heyday of Nantucket, the island's harbor bristled with the masts of whalers and other sailing ships. 47

*B*rant Point Light, on Nantucket, echoes the crimson glow of sunrise. A
nearby fisherman accompanied by his dog tries for an early morning catch.
Nantucketers built the first lighthouse here in 1746, after the island's whaling
industry began to develop. As catches in the Atlantic declined, the whalers rounded
Cape Horn on long Pacific voyages. Above, Nantucketers play pinochle in the
Pacific Club, an organization founded in 1854 by whaling ship captains. Pictures
of early members hang on the wall. The building housing the Pacific Club,
constructed in 1772, once served as the countinghouse and headquarters for
whaling entrepreneur William Rotch, principal owner of the ship Beaver.
Returning from London in 1773 with a load of tea, the Beaver and two other
vessels anchored in Boston Harbor. On the night of December 16, American
rebels masquerading as Indians dumped the tea overboard in protest against British
trade policies—the event since celebrated as the Boston Tea Party.

*T*hickets of huckleberry and scrub oak carpet a moor in muted autumn shades in Nantucket's interior. Once considered unsuitable for building lots, such land remained held in common by the First Purchasers—the original white settlers of Nantucket. This communal system lasted from 1659 to 1816, when a mainland court overturned it in favor of private ownership. At right, a house built in the lean-to style of the late 17th century catches the last rays of sunlight. Many Nantucketers build their homes in styles that reflect the island's heritage.

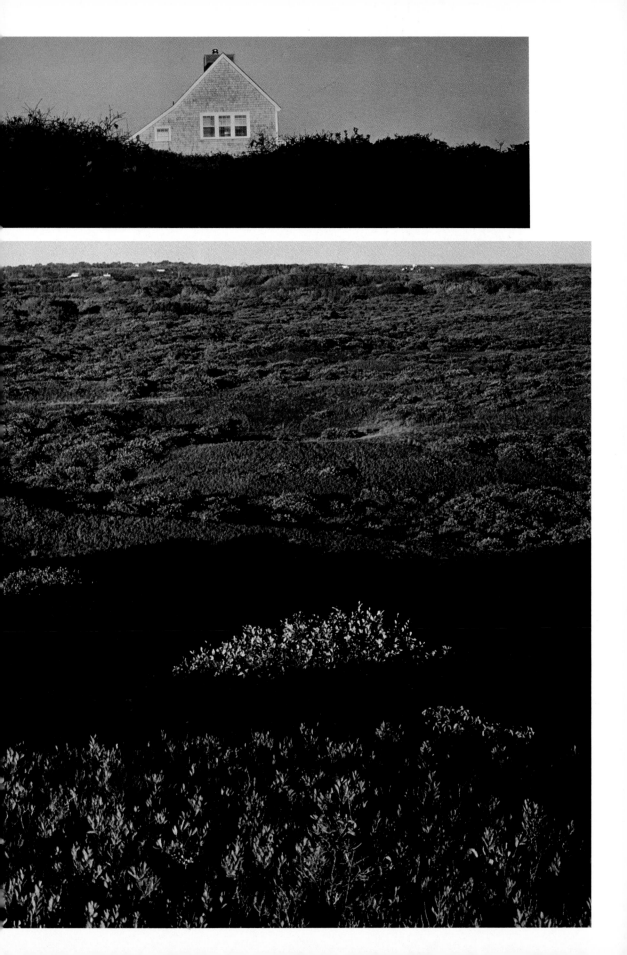

*G*ilded eagle figurehead spreads its wings above clouds of salt spray as the sailing vessel Shenandoah heels to starboard. The square topsail schooner carries passengers on six-day cruises throughout the summer, sailing each Monday from her home port of Vineyard Haven, on Martha's Vineyard. Below, passengers and crew strain on a halyard; passengers often volunteer to help with shipboard duties. With the ship under way, passenger Mary Maynard (bottom) relaxes with a novel atop the after cabin. Captain Robert S. Douglas allowed few concessions to modernity in the construction of his ship. The Shenandoah, launched in 1964, remains true to the design of her 19th-century predecessors.

*H*igh above the deck, 8-year-old Jamie Douglas playfully grabs
for a grease can dangling from deckhand Jim Kricker's bosun's
chair. The son of Captain Douglas, Jamie scampered up the rigging
of the ship like a veteran sailor. The coating of grease Kricker applies
lubricates and helps preserve the mast. Below, the passenger schooner Bill
of Rights trails the Shenandoah as the two ships sail together off Vineyard
Haven Harbor. Until the early 1900s, thousands of such vessels plied the
waters along the East Coast. Today, only a few commercial sailing vessels
remain, carrying passengers or serving as training ships.

Riding a wall of water, 14-year-old Bryan Harvey surges toward South Beach, on Martha's

Vineyard. Public beaches here offer surf, sand, and sun for thousands of visitors annually.

Friends of ours from Washington, D. C., David and Alexa Zimmerman, had joined my wife, Meredith, and me on Nantucket for a week's vacation. David and Alexa decided to have a quarter board made bearing the address of their suburban Virginia home. I accompanied David when he visited woodworker Abram Niles in his backyard shop.

A heavyset man with deliberate speech, Niles was wearing sawdust-sprinkled work clothes when we arrived. After he had jotted down the details of size, color, design, and spelling for David and Alexa's quarter board, Niles talked with us for a few moments. He told us that as a young man, he had served in a lifesaving unit of the U. S. Coast Guard, and he invited us to see the island's lifesaving museum the following Saturday, when he would be on duty as a guide.

Several days later David and I drove northeastward from Nantucket town on our way to visit the museum. The road we traveled, Polpis Road, dipped and rolled as it ran through fields and moorland. The sight of the gently rolling land brought to mind how this 45-square-mile island was formed. When the last Ice Age glacier that covered New England began receding, it released the burden of rock and sand it had carried and pushed before it. It was the accumulation of this debris that produced Nantucket and other islands in this region.

Arriving at the lifesaving museum, David and I parked near the contemporary building, a replica of Surfside Station, the island's first lifesaving station. Inside, Abram Niles greeted us. He now wore an immaculately pressed khaki uniform with the insignias of the old U. S. Life-Saving Service—a forerunner of the Coast Guard—gleaming from each collar point. As we walked through the small museum's single display room, Abram pointed out a surfboat similar to those used for rescue attempts on Nantucket. We also saw quarter boards from vessels that had been wrecked off the island, as well as photographs of the men of the Life-Saving Service.

"There was a tradition in the service," Abram told us, "that its members would not hesitate to risk their lives to save others. As one Life-Saving Service officer is supposed to have said, 'The regulations say only that you have to go out; they don't say you have to come back.'"

Later that same day I stood at the rail of the ferry bound for Cape Cod. As I looked back at Nantucket, I thought of Abram Niles and the other Nantucketers I had met. Mindful of their heritage, these people seem glad to share it with others even as they strive to preserve it. I recalled then what one Nantucketer had told me. "We're proud of our island," the young woman had said with the conviction of one born and brought up on Nantucket. "It's a beautiful place with a fascinating history, and we enjoy visitors who share our appreciation of our island."

*A*s I looked across the harbor at Vineyard Haven, on Martha's Vineyard, I saw a large sailing vessel rolling gently at anchor. The ship was the *Shenandoah*, a topsail schooner that takes passengers on six-day cruises. I had come to sail aboard the *Shenandoah* to catch the flavor of earlier days, when schooners plied the waters about these islands. Meredith and I arrived at Vineyard Haven the evening before the *Shenandoah* was to sail. The ship's yawl boat ferried us and our luggage to where she lay on her mooring. Shortly after we boarded, we sat with several other newly arrived passengers in the main cabin while First Mate Bill Mabie welcomed us aboard.

After explaining a few details of shipboard life, he concluded by saying that although the *Shenandoah* carried no engine, a small diesel-powered generator would be run from seven-thirty to eight o'clock each morning to recharge the batteries that powered interior lights, navigation equipment, and the washdown pump.

"When you hear the generator start," he said, "be sure your portholes are closed. That's when we hose down the decks, and if you leave your portholes open, you may find yourself sleeping in a wet bed." Later in the cruise, the noisy generator prompted one passenger to remark that if he ever got homesick for the *Shenandoah* he would have someone start his lawn mower outside his bedroom window at seven-thirty in the morning. He would certainly dream that he was on board again!

We spent the first morning aboard ship sitting in Vineyard Haven Harbor, waiting for the right combination of wind and tide. When we were ready to hoist sail shortly after lunch, the first mate explained how the passengers could help raise the mainsail. We nervously joined the crew, lining up along thick manila halyards at port and starboard. At the

Shuttle in hand, Andy Oates of Nantucket Looms weaves custom fabric using wool and linen yarn and strips of cotton. Part owner of Nantucket Looms, Oates has thirty years' experience as a weaver. Shops such as his help keep alive handicrafts on Nantucket.

command, "Haul away," we all grasped the line and pulled hand over hand with all our might. "Hold that!" meant for us to stop pulling and brace ourselves to hold the line taut. At the command, "Up behind!" everyone dropped the line—"Like a hot potato," the first mate shouted—and crew members made the line fast.

I had never before traveled aboard a sailing vessel as large as the *Shenandoah*. She was 108 feet long at the rail, and her masts towered 94 feet above the water. Although I knew that larger ships had relied on wind power, it was nonetheless thrilling for me to realize that only the wind and tide were driving us as we picked up speed and slipped silently out of Vineyard Haven Harbor.

At the helm of the *Shenandoah* stood Captain Robert S. Douglas, shipowner and master. A tall, red-haired man, he squinted into the bright sunlight as he checked the sails. When someone asked the captain about our destination, he gave a vague reply, but word spread that we were bound for Nantucket. Later that afternoon, however, shifting winds and tides that ran against us slowed our progress. We turned back and anchored that evening in Edgartown Harbor, on Martha's Vineyard, about eight miles from where we had sailed that afternoon.

Next morning, the weather favored us with a fair breeze. We made a glorious run to Nantucket, every sail spread and the ship heeling over until her scuppers were awash. With the wind humming in the rigging, the ship's sails billowed in the breeze. Her plunging bow threw spray over the deck as the graceful schooner sliced through the dark water.

Those days under sail illustrated a point that Captain Douglas wanted to emphasize to all his passengers. "Nearly all of us live where we can just jump in the car and go wherever we wish without a second thought about the weather," the captain told me one afternoon. "I want to remind people that life was not always like that. For countless centuries, seafarers had to know and depend on the winds and the tides. I want to make people aware," he concluded, "of the natural world about them, even if only in a small way."

When we returned to Martha's Vineyard after our cruise aboard the *Shenandoah*, traffic jammed the streets of Edgartown. A former whaling port, Edgartown was the first white settlement on the hundred-square-mile island. We had arrived during Regatta Week, and celebrating boaters were everywhere. Seeing the enthusiastic throng brought home to me the importance of tourism to this island.

Martha's Vineyard has a year-round population of about 10,000 people. In summer, an additional 55,000 people stay here—not counting the thousands who ride the ferry from the mainland for the day. But however busy the island towns may be, a short walk or bicycle ride outside the downtown areas leaves the crowds behind. Nowhere is this contrast more striking than in the town of Oak Bluffs.

Located on the north coastal road east of Vineyard Haven, Oak Bluffs is burdened by heavy automobile traffic during summer. Its business district is full of activity, and lines form outside the entrances of popular restaurants even at lunchtime. Yet just a block from the busy harbor area lies a peaceful, quiet community, a community filled with homes distinguished by their Victorian gingerbread ornaments.

This area is the site of the Martha's Vineyard Camp-Meeting Association, a group that traces its beginnings to 1835, when the first camp meeting here was held by Methodists on the site of present-day Oak Bluffs. In 1851 more than 3,500 people attended Sunday services during camp meeting week. A hundred tents set up on the grounds housed many of these people. Within five years the number of tents had doubled, and by 1858 the first wooden houses, small enough to fit on a single tent lot, were built.

In a frenzy of decoration, owners added scrollwork, scalloped shingles, tiny balconies, turrets, and distinctive arched windows. Then they painted the cottages in rainbow hues. One current resident remarked

Free-form sandbar off the tip of Tuckernuck Island reflects the ceaseless changes wrought by the sea. Waves, currents, and storms have built up parts of the sandbar and eroded others. In a matter of months such formations can present completely different profiles. The same forces at work here affect many of the islands along the Atlantic shore. At lower right, a small plane flies near the sandbar.

jokingly that it seemed as if those early owners were simultaneously attempting to exceed both the decorative efforts of their neighbors and the bounds of good taste. Some 300 cottages remain today on the camp meeting grounds. Strolling along the tranquil, shady streets here is like walking through a colorful 1890s valentine.

"We enjoy our summers here because the community is family oriented," Walter Frey told Meredith and me as we sat on the front porch of the Frey's cottage, Small Frey. Walter and his lovely wife, Beryl, had invited us to join them for the annual celebration known as Illumination Night. First celebrated in 1869, Illumination Night soon became an annual event in the community. Preparations for this year's celebration were nearly complete when we arrived at the Freys' home. Oriental lanterns were hung from every conceivable point of attachment, from porches, windows, trees—even from picket fences.

As darkness began to fall, we strolled with Beryl across the lawn of Trinity Park to the Tabernacle, the focal point of the camp meeting grounds. A large round iron structure, the Tabernacle was built in 1879 to replace a circus tent that had previously sheltered worshipers. I noticed that the canvas sides of the Tabernacle, usually pulled back, were closed tonight. The evening's program began with singing. Philip O. Buddington, program director for the Tabernacle, led with such infectious enthusiasm that the 2,000 people inside made the building ring.

After the brief program, the lights in the Tabernacle were dimmed. Oak Bluffs' oldest resident, Edith McCarthy, born a century ago, was the guest of honor. She was invited to light the first of the lanterns. As the first light flickered gaily, the announcement rang out, "Let the lanterns be lit." At that moment, a gasp of wonder ran through the audience as ushers drew back the canvas sides of the Tabernacle. All around us, a riot of light and color blazed from the houses, growing in intensity as more and more lanterns were lit.

"This is the ninth illumination I've seen," our friend Beryl Frey told us quietly, "and it still takes my breath away."

Important as tourism is to Martha's Vineyard, it is not the island's sole source of income. Fishing provides a living for some residents. The village of Menemsha, near the western end of the island, remains a working fishing village—although today its picturesque boathouses and fishing shacks attract painters and photographers.

Another reminder of the importance of fishing on the island is the Massachusetts State Lobster Hatchery and Research Station, located on the lagoon between Oak Bluffs and Vineyard Haven. Inside the hatchery's cool, white-painted hatching room visitors can observe egg-bearing lobsters. The female lobsters are caught in the wild, usually in April and May. They are held until their eggs hatch in June or July.

The fry, as the larval lobsters are called, are transferred to containers around the sides of the room as soon as they hatch. Panels on the

walls depict how the fry molt four times before they begin to look like tiny lobsters. "Until the fourth molt, which takes about a month, the fry simply drift in the water," John T. Hughes, the director of the hatchery, told me. "Thus they are extremely vulnerable. Here at the hatchery we keep them safe from predators during those stages, although we still lose many because lobsters are cannibalistic.

"Of every 10,000 fry hatched here, 3,000 to 4,000 survive those critical first stages and are released into the sea. Now, a survival rate of about one-third may not sound like a success at first, until you consider this. In the wild, we estimate that of 10,000 fry hatched, only *one* will survive that long.

"We're conducting research here at the hatchery to gain more information about lobsters and to develop ways of growing them commercially, which will help supplement their diminishing numbers," Hughes continued. "For example, in the sea a lobster takes about seven or eight years to grow to maturity. Here in the laboratory, by providing abundant

Lullaby cottage lives up to its name: Owner Joseph Berry naps on his front porch in the Martha's Vineyard town of Oak Bluffs. Lullaby and other nearby homes, built in the mid-19th century, replaced tents once used during summer gatherings of the Martha's Vineyard Camp-Meeting Association.

food and keeping the water warm the year round, we've grown mature lobsters in less than two years. As a result of our research," he stated, "I believe that commercial lobster farming will soon be practical."

While farming the sea may contribute to the economy of Martha's Vineyard in the future, farming the land has been important in its past. Even before the first English farms were established in 1642, Wampanoag Indians grew corn and other vegetables on the island. Relations between the Indians and the English remained generally cordial during the period of settlement. Most of the Indians were converted to Christianity, and as early as 1665 one of them entered Harvard University.

In 1870 the Indian town of Gay Head was incorporated on Martha's Vineyard. The town takes its name from the nearby cliffs of varicolored clay. "Gay Head is what Niagara would be," wrote Daniel Webster in 1849, "if instead of 150 feet of falling water, it exhibited a perpendicular bank of that height, composed of lines, strata, and sections of various earths and highly contrasted colors."

The cliffs, threatened by erosion, have been designated a national landmark. No longer can souvenir-seekers carve out a piece of the bright clay. Instead, an overlook offers a panoramic view of the magnificently colored cliffs. To reach the viewpoint, visitors must walk through a small area of gift shops and refreshment stands. In one of these gift shops I met Charles W. Vanderhoop, the vice-chairman of the Gay Head Tribal Council. His rich, coppery skin, dark eyes, and straight black hair testify to his Wampanoag ancestry.

"My family has lived here on the Vineyard," he told me, "since before there were written records. My father was in the Coast Guard, and later served as keeper of the Gay Head Lighthouse. I myself have been going to sea for thirty years." An experienced captain, Charles takes command of a ship every winter and has been around the world many times. "When I am at sea, my family lives on the mainland," he told me. "It's more convenient for them in the winter. But every summer we return to Gay Head to live and to run our gift shop."

Charles said he has seen many changes in Gay Head over the years. "I can remember, as recently as thirty years ago, when almost everyone living here was Indian. Today we have nearly every ethnic group represented in our community, and the number of summer people is increasing. Thus we face the same problems the other island towns face.

"In effect, Gay Head has two communities," he concluded. "Those who live here all year and work here, and those—many of them city people—who live here during the summer or vacation here. As you would expect, the two groups don't always share the same values."

Several days later, as I prepared to leave Martha's Vineyard, I thought of Charles Vanderhoop again, and I realized that he represents an unusual blending of interests. A native Vineyarder whose ancestors have lived on the island for generations, Charles earns much of his living from the sea. Yet, as the proprietor of a gift shop, he also gains from the influx of visitors to his island.

Suddenly I remembered what Charles had told me when we were speaking about the relationship between the island's full-time residents and its summer visitors. "What we all have to realize," he had said, "is that there must be understanding on both sides. The two cultures here have to mesh, not collide."

*G*ingerbread ornaments and festive colors accent cottages on the grounds of the Martha's Vineyard Camp-Meeting Association. At the first summer meeting here, held in 1835, Methodist ministers conducted services in the open air; they and their followers lived in nine tents. The popularity of the meetings grew through the years, and in 1858 more than 12,000 people attended Sunday services. At that time people began to replace their tents with cottages. Eventually hundreds of these homes filled the camp meeting grounds. During Illumination Night, candles glow inside oriental lanterns (right) hung about the porch of Small Frey, the summer home of the Walter Frey family. Originally held to celebrate the last night of camp meeting, Illumination Night has become an annual highlight of the summer season in Oak Bluffs.

*W*atercolor smile brightens an apprehensive face at the Martha's Vineyard Agricultural Society's Live Stock Show and Fair. The three-day island fair, held each August in West Tisbury, attracts both summer visitors and year-round residents. The face-painting booth raises money for a local preschool. During the crosscut sawing contest (below), sawdust flies as competitors vie for the Massachusetts State Woodsmen's Championship. At an evening performance, a young musician (below, right) entertains fairgoers during the fiddlers' contest.

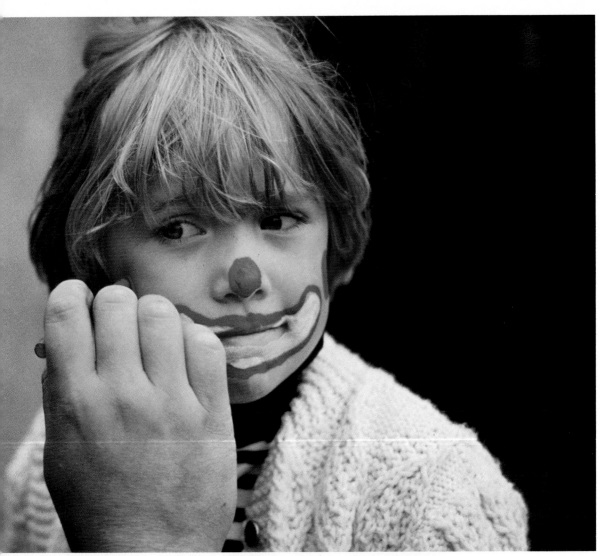

With the slate-blue Atlantic beckoning a short distance ahead, summer residents of Martha's

Vineyard head down a sandy lane toward a private beach on the southern shore of the island.

Island Jewels in

Crews silhouetted against sun-gilded sails, the yachts Freedom, *left,* and Australia *ghost across*

an Urban Setting By H. Robert Morrison

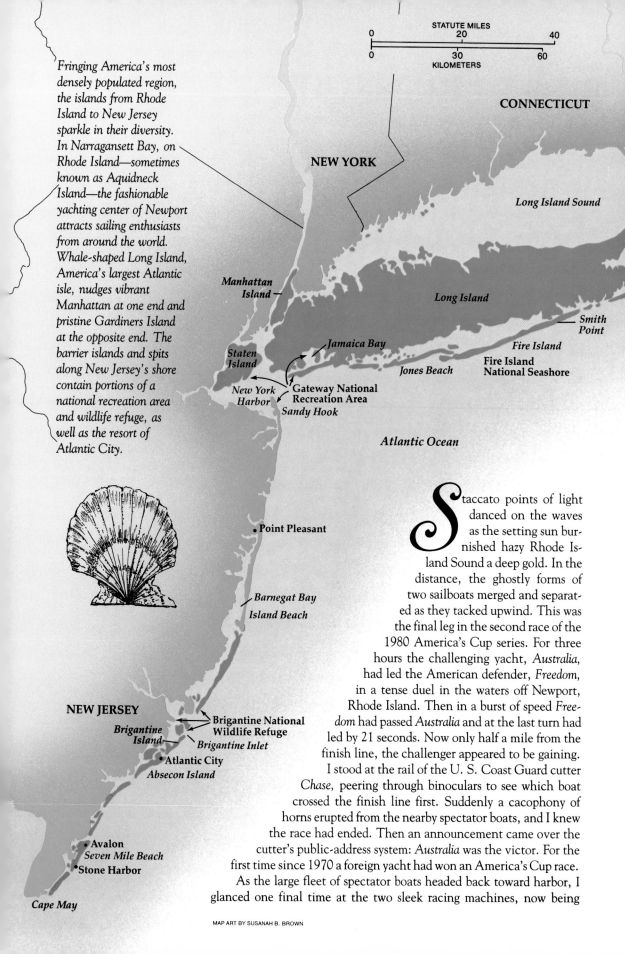

Fringing America's most
densely populated region,
the islands from Rhode
Island to New Jersey
sparkle in their diversity.
In Narragansett Bay, on
Rhode Island—sometimes
known as Aquidneck
Island—the fashionable
yachting center of Newport
attracts sailing enthusiasts
from around the world.
Whale-shaped Long Island,
America's largest Atlantic
isle, nudges vibrant
Manhattan at one end and
pristine Gardiners Island
at the opposite end. The
barrier islands and spits
along New Jersey's shore
contain portions of a
national recreation area
and wildlife refuge, as
well as the resort of
Atlantic City.

STATUTE MILES

0   20   40

0   30   60
KILOMETERS

CONNECTICUT

NEW YORK

Long Island Sound

Manhattan
Island —

Long Island

Smith
Point

Jamaica Bay

Fire Island

Staten
Island

Fire Island
National Seashore

Jones Beach

New York
Harbor

Gateway National
Recreation Area

Sandy Hook

Atlantic Ocean

• Point Pleasant

Barnegat Bay
Island Beach

NEW JERSEY

Brigantine
Island —

Brigantine National
Wildlife Refuge

Brigantine Inlet

• Atlantic City
Absecon Island

• Avalon
Seven Mile Beach
• Stone Harbor

Cape May

Staccato points of light
danced on the waves
as the setting sun bur-
nished hazy Rhode Is-
land Sound a deep gold. In the
distance, the ghostly forms of
two sailboats merged and separated as they tacked upwind. This was
the final leg in the second race of the
1980 America's Cup series. For three
hours the challenging yacht, *Australia*,
had led the American defender, *Freedom*,
in a tense duel in the waters off Newport,
Rhode Island. Then in a burst of speed *Freedom* had passed *Australia* and at the last turn had
led by 21 seconds. Now only half a mile from the
finish line, the challenger appeared to be gaining.
I stood at the rail of the U. S. Coast Guard cutter
Chase, peering through binoculars to see which boat
crossed the finish line first. Suddenly a cacophony of
horns erupted from the nearby spectator boats, and I knew
the race had ended. Then an announcement came over the
cutter's public-address system: *Australia* was the victor. For the
first time since 1970 a foreign yacht had won an America's Cup race.
As the large fleet of spectator boats headed back toward harbor, I
glanced one final time at the two sleek racing machines, now being

MASS.

Narragansett Bay

RHODE ISLAND

Newport

Rhode Island (Aquidneck Island)

Rhode Island Sound

Plum Island

Gardiners Island

Gardiners Bay

Montauk Point

Montauk

towed by their tenders. The sailboats' streamlined hulls, some sixty feet long, were topped by masts more than eighty feet high. I marveled at the beauty of these boats and at the dedication that drives the men who build and race them.

Although *Australia*'s victory this day evened the best-of-seven series at one win each, the America's Cup was to remain secure, for *Freedom* won the next three races handily. *Freedom*'s successful defense of the Cup perpetuated the unbroken string of U. S. victories. Since the yacht *America* brought home the trophy from Britain in 1851, the America's Cup has rested safely with the New York Yacht Club.

Darkness had fallen by the time the cutter eased into its berth. As I walked past the harbor at Newport, lights glittered cheerily from the hundreds of boats moored there. Laughter and music echoed from the countless parties that were under way on the decks of gleaming sailboats and power cruisers. Looking around me, I savored the atmosphere that is found only in international yachting centers such as Newport.

Located at the mouth of Narragansett Bay on the island that shares the name of the state, Newport has been the site of the America's Cup races 11 times since 1930. In addition to its fame as a yachting mecca, the city is known for its music festivals. But despite the large crowds drawn to Newport by such events, the city retains an air of elegance and gentility. Perhaps this reflects the origins of the state of Rhode Island.

Rhode Island began as an experiment in religious liberty. In 1636 the outspoken minister Roger Williams was banished from Puritan Massachusetts because of his religious views. Williams moved to what is now the state of Rhode Island and established the town of Providence, one of the first major communities in the world to advocate religious freedom. Other colonies tolerated varied forms of Christianity, but only Rhode Island offered freedom to worshipers of all faiths. The adoption in 1791 of similar guarantees in the First Amendment to the United States Constitution confirmed the success of the Rhode Island experiment.

Today a testimony to this early spirit of religious liberty stands on a quiet tree-shaded street in Newport: Touro Synagogue, the oldest existing synagogue in the United States. Built according to plans drawn by noted colonial architect Peter Harrison, Touro Synagogue was dedicated in 1763. Its exterior of plain buff brick contrasts with the richness of its Georgian interior. Inside the synagogue, a dozen columns represent the 12 tribes of ancient Israel, and five massive brass candelabra hang under the domed three-story-high ceiling.

A few blocks away from Touro Synagogue stands another of Newport's many examples of colonial architecture, Trinity Church. The soaring white steeple of this Episcopal church, surmounted by a bishop's miter, has dominated Newport's skyline ever since it was built. Completed in 1726, the church was enlarged in 1762.

My wife, Meredith, and I were fortunate to have as our guide there Canon John D. Zimmerman. "These pews," Canon Zimmerman told us inside Trinity's sanctuary, "were built enclosed in boxes not so much for privacy as for warmth. As you can see, the interiors of many of the boxes

display a variety of carpeting and upholstery. This reflects the practice, common among Anglican families of the day, of buying a pew and decorating it according to one's purse and taste. Thus, although the parish owned the church, many of the pews were owned by individuals. Even today, two of Trinity's pews remain in private hands. Trinity Church has been cared for lovingly," Canon Zimmerman concluded. "For the most part, it appears today as it did in the 18th century."

Another reminder of Newport's past is a small stone building not far from Trinity Church. This is the armory of the Newport Artillery Company. The company traces its origins to 1741, when it was chartered by King George II. The company remains in existence as one of the oldest military units in the United States; today its functions are ceremonial. Dressed in authentic colonial costumes, its members serve as honor guards at civic events.

The armory, now a museum, houses such company relics as a letter from George Washington. Its major attraction, though, is an astonishing collection of military uniforms, not only from the United States armed forces, but also from military units around the world.

"When I began working for the museum in 1960, we didn't have any foreign pieces," Lt. Col. Elton M. Manuel, the curator, told me. Colonel Manuel, a short man with an erect military bearing, accompanied me through the museum. His stories poured forth in an enthusiastic verbal barrage as he pointed out favorite exhibits with his cane.

"I got the idea that perhaps some military leaders might donate uniforms to us," he said, "and so I wangled postage money from the artillery company and mailed out some letters. The first response came from Sir Bernard Law Montgomery, who served as the World War II British commander in North Africa. Why, his uniform came in so fast I'd swear Monty was out in the backyard with it wrapped and in his hands when he got my letter," Colonel Manuel concluded with a laugh.

Over the years, Newport has experienced several fluctuations in its level of prosperity. Shortly after the Revolution, the port city entered a

Boats roll gently in the harbor of Newport, Rhode Island, as reflected sunlight burns golden in waterfront windows. The steeple of St. Mary's Church, where John and Jacqueline Kennedy were married in 1953, towers above the masts of the sailboats. Newport's location at the entrance to Narragansett Bay makes the city an ideal stopover for boats cruising along the coast.

period of decline. But the town's fortunes began rising again in the mid-1800s with its discovery by vacationers. Among these were a number of southern planters who sought a location with cool weather during summer. By 1860 summering in Newport had become fashionable, and cottages were springing up on the onetime farmland east of town.

Cottages these dwellings were, but strictly in the New England sense of the word: any home, however large, that was lived in only part of the year. The largest of Newport's cottages, The Breakers, contains some seventy rooms. It was completed in 1895 by Cornelius Vanderbilt to replace a more modest mansion destroyed by fire. He spared no expense to make this home an opulent showpiece. The mansion was built by an army of laborers and craftsmen—many of them brought to Newport from Europe.

One afternoon Meredith and I joined a group of visitors in The Breakers, which is now owned by The Preservation Society of Newport County. As our guide led us through room after room, all beautifully furnished, I could imagine the mansion filled with elegantly dressed men and women whiling away carefree summer evenings.

Many of the parties held in such mansions were deliberately planned to enhance their hostess's position in the Four Hundred—the list of "acceptable" high society. Mere ostentation soon became commonplace at these parties, and elaborate costume balls passé. To secure the coveted attention of their neighbors, the grand dames of Newport turned to novelty. One party was held in which the guest list included a hundred dogs—all from the very best families, of course!

Southwest of Newport lies New York's Long Island, the largest of America's Atlantic isles. Its population of 6.7 million is greater than the individual populations of 41 states. Because of its size, Long Island possesses a character far different from that of any of the other coastal islands. Indeed, it has its own offshore isles, and it was several of these smaller islands that I decided to visit.

The first such island I visited, Plum Island, lies just off the northeastern tip of Long Island. It is the site of the U. S. Department of Agriculture's Plum Island Animal Disease Center. My guide on the island was Dr. Jonathan Richmond, the center's biological safety officer.

As a safety measure, no one is permitted on Plum Island without the permission of the federal government. Dr. Richmond impressed upon me the care that is taken to prevent the spread of diseases from the center's laboratory. "When Congress passed the legislation establishing this laboratory," Dr. Richmond explained, "one requirement was that it be located on a coastal island to help prevent the accidental spread of disease to the mainland.

"Our mission here is threefold—research, diagnosis, and training," Dr. Richmond continued. "We do basic research on how foreign animal diseases spread and how they can be controlled. We also work to discover tests for diagnosing diseases and to develop vaccines for controlling them. Since these diseases are foreign, U. S. veterinarians generally never have an opportunity to study them firsthand. Our training programs are important," he concluded, "because they enable veterinarians to identify these diseases and prevent expensive loss of livestock."

After talking with Dr. Richmond and other scientists on Plum Island—men and women who are looking to the future—it was a contrast to meet a man rooted in the past. Robert David Lion Gardiner is a tenth-generation American whose family came to the New World nearly three and a half centuries ago. Gardiners Island, at the eastern end of Long Island, has been in his family's possession since it was acquired in 1639.

"The first Gardiner in North America was Lion Gardiner," Robert told Meredith and me when we visited him in his palatial home in East Hampton, New York. An energetic 70-year-old with piercing hazel eyes, Robert cannot resist sharing his passion for the historic connections between his family and the New World. "Lion was a military engineer, the first to visit the colonies. He arrived in 1635 with his Dutch wife, Mary, and a maid. They had a four-year contract from the English government that guaranteed their passage back to England.

"*L*ion strengthened Boston's defenses, including fortifications on Breed's Hill and Bunker Hill—where rebellious colonists fought the British nearly a century and a half later," Robert continued, speaking of his 17th-century ancestor with the familiarity one might use in referring to a contemporary cousin. "He also built and commanded Saybrook Fort at the mouth of the Connecticut River, on the mainland just a short distance across Long Island Sound from Gardiners Island.

"Near the end of his four-year contract, Lion decided that he would rather stay in North America than face the perilous voyage home. He had chosen Gardiners Island—then known as the Isle of Wight—as the place where he wanted to live, and so he began negotiations with Wyandanch, the sachem of the Montauk Indians. The Montauks called the island Manchonake—Island of Death—because of the wars and pestilence they experienced there. Lion bought the island from the Indians for 'ten coats of trading cloth' and a few sundries. On the deed Lion wrote, Wyandanch signed by drawing stick figures with hands joined, a symbol of friendship between Indians and whites."

As we prepared to leave his East Hampton home for a visit to Gardiners Island, Robert hardly paused in his story. "About this same time Lion had applied for and received a royal grant to the island from the crown. Lion's position was that of a baron," he said, "because his grant gave him nearly complete control of the island."

Robert then explained that during this period there were disputes between the Dutch and the English over the New World territories. "You see, the Dutch had already settled on Long Island. However, Gardiners Island was claimed by the English. The English crown was happy to have Lion settle Gardiners Island because it was interested in having an outpost near the Dutch colony. Lion died in 1663, a year before New Amsterdam was taken by the English and renamed New York."

At the marina where Robert keeps his boat, we were joined by Mary and Hugo Mutz, friends of the Gardiners. Hugo took the helm of Robert's speedy motor launch, and we cast off on a journey into another era. "One of the advantages of living on the island was its closeness to the centers of commerce," Robert remarked as we cut through the calm waters of Gardiners Bay. "For generations Gardiners Island was one night's sail from New York City," he explained, "while to get to New York City by land from East Hampton, on Long Island, required a trip of four days by horse and coach."

When we arrived at Gardiners Island, Hugo sat behind the wheel of a pickup truck, and Robert climbed into the back with Mary, Meredith, and me for a tour of the 3,300-acre island, which today looks much as it did centuries ago. Wildlife abounds on the island: We saw deer, wild turkeys, ospreys, and large flocks of Canada geese. About the only signs of human habitation are the brick mansion, a few outbuildings, a grass airstrip, and a white-painted windmill.

"The arms of the windmill," Robert told us, "once served to signal Long Island. When they were stopped diagonally, like the letter X, it meant that the coast was clear. When the arms were set vertically

Skipper Dennis Conner mans the helm of Freedom, *the 1980 defender of the America's Cup. The boat heads for the starting line of the 24.3-mile racecourse off Newport. Conner practiced for more than a year with his handpicked crew, among them, left to right, Halsey Herreshoff, John Marshall, and Dennis Durgan. Their preparation paid off.* Freedom *won the best-of-seven series four races to one.*

and horizontally, like a cross, they warned of the presence of pirates."

"Pirates were a definite menace," Robert said as we drove along one of the dirt roads that crisscross the island. We had entered a shady forest, a reminder of the large forests that once covered Long Island. Wild grapevines hung from the gnarled limbs of great oak trees, some of them centuries old. A deer started ahead of us and ran down the road for a short distance before bounding off into the undergrowth.

Suddenly Robert tapped the cab of the truck with his hand. He called out for Hugo to stop, then said, "Come with me. I'll show you where Captain Kidd buried his treasure." As we walked a little way down an overgrown track, Robert told us a tale about the famous pirate. "Captain Kidd once visited John Gardiner, the third Lord of the Manor. The reason Kidd visited John Gardiner was that he wanted to hide some treasure on John's property. Kidd sent the loot ashore, where it was buried. Before he left, he warned John, 'If I come back and this treasure is not here, I will have your head—or your son's.'

"It was not long before Kidd was captured in Boston and taken to London, where he was later hanged. John, meanwhile, was biding his time. He knew that if the pirate escaped, he might return. If Kidd found the treasure disturbed he would not hesitate to carry out his threat. In the end, John's caution paid off. After Kidd was captured, the Earl of Bellomont—the English governor of the colonies of New York, New Hampshire, and Massachusetts Bay—discovered a note in the pirate's journal that gave the location of the treasure. *(Continued on page 84)*

*C*lose-hauled on a port tack, Freedom *pounds across the finish line 3 minutes 38 seconds ahead of the challenger,* Australia. *Raw New England fall weather, with typically strong winds, gave the edge to the American yacht. However, one crew member admitted the Americans could have been beaten had different wind conditions prevailed. Spurred by the urge to end the United States' 110-year domination of the America's Cup races, the Australians used a new bendable mast that gave them greater speed in light wind conditions. Their colorful spinnakers ballooning in the wind (right), the 12-Meter yachts test their skilled crews to the utmost as the boats sail close together on a reaching leg. Almost immediately after* Freedom's *victory, challenges emerged for the next races. Yacht clubs in Australia, France, Britain, Canada, Sweden, and Italy have announced they will try to wrest the Cup from American hands in 1983.*

*M*onument to the Gilded Age—the decades around the turn of the century—the Newport "summer cottage" known as The Breakers (top) reflects an era of baronial splendor. The late 1800s saw Newport emerge as a glittering summer resort for members of the Four Hundred, the elite of society. Cornelius Vanderbilt, grandson and namesake of railroad tycoon Commodore Cornelius Vanderbilt, employed architect Richard Morris Hunt to design The Breakers in the style of Renaissance palaces of Italy. Of its 70 rooms, 35 housed the servants necessary to support the lavish entertaining of hostess Alice Vanderbilt. The 45-foot-high Great Hall (above) features carved stone imported from France. Crystal chandeliers, marble columns, and allegorical ceiling paintings embellish the mansion's dining room (right).

Immensity of sea and sky dwarfs a solitary figure at Montauk, on Long Island. Busy

Manhattan lies just 120 miles from nearby Montauk Point, easternmost tip of New York State.

"Now, the original grant of land did not include mineral rights. All silver and gold found on the island belonged to the crown. And thus the treasure slipped from the grasp of John Gardiner. The Earl of Bellomont sent for John and ordered him to bring the treasure with him to Boston."

We stopped at a small marker, hardly noticeable in the undergrowth. With a dramatic gesture, Robert announced: "This is the very spot where the treasure was found. The cache they dug up contained gold, silver, diamonds, sapphires, and Indian brocades. It's all listed on a receipt the Earl gave John Gardiner. The treasure was auctioned off in London. The proceeds went to purchase a residence for the governor of London's Greenwich Hospital."

Robert's tale of the treasure had one further twist. "When I visited England several years ago," he told me, "I took a copy of my ancestor's receipt with me and compared it with the one the Earl had sent back to England. Mine matched the Earl's in every respect, with one exception: The English document listed six fewer diamonds than did John Gardiner's receipt. Apparently," Robert said with a laugh, "the Earl decided to compensate himself by pocketing six of the jewels."

Leaving the site of Captain Kidd's treasure, we walked back to the truck and continued our tour. As we drove along, Robert told us that he has no children and that he shares Gardiners Island with other heirs. He mentioned that disputes have arisen about the present-day use of the island and about its future.

"What I want to do is purchase the island completely and set up a nonprofit foundation to care for it," he said. "Only limited numbers of naturalists and historians would be permitted to visit here.

"The island must remain the priceless repository of human and natural history it is today," Robert concluded. "Unlimited public access would soon destroy Gardiners Island."

I found similar feelings about public access expressed by some residents of the next island I visited: Fire Island, a sandy strip of land south of Long Island and the site of Fire Island National Seashore. The environment of Fire Island was a distinct change from that of the islands Meredith and I had visited earlier. Actually a large sandbar averaging about two-tenths of a mile in width, Fire Island was the first true barrier island we would visit.

Barrier islands are given their name because they serve as buffers between the mainland and the ocean, moderating the effects of tides and storms. These low, sandy islands extend from Massachusetts all the way to Texas. Fire Island came into being as the last Ice Age glacier receded. It was formed by wave-created currents that eroded the eastern end of Long Island, then deposited the sand along its southern shore.

Today 17 diverse communities dot the 32-mile length of Fire Island, stretched along a single unpaved track nicknamed the "Burma Road." Two bridges connect the thin strip of sand with Long Island. Early during my visit to Fire Island I talked with Joel Pickelner, superintendent of the national seashore. A handsome, athletic young man with dark hair and dark eyes, he lives on the island year round with his wife and family. As we chatted, I mentioned to him that I felt Fire Island contains the finest beach I have visited in the United States. "Because the island is aligned east-and-west," Joel explained, "the beach gets direct sunshine all day long. That's why it's so superb for sunbathing.

"Fire Island has something for every vacationer," Joel continued. "For the day visitor who likes a lot of company and doesn't want to take a ferry, Smith Point near the eastern end of the island offers access by bridge and has lifeguards and a large parking lot.

"If you like seclusion, walk a short distance in either direction from almost any of the communities on the island and you'll pretty much have the beach to yourself. And one section of eastern Fire Island has remained so untouched that it has been designated a wilderness area."

Most visitors to Fire Island arrive by boat, either on privately

Heir to a historic isle, Robert David Lion Gardiner strides along a lane leading from the family manor house. His family has owned Gardiners Island, located near the eastern tip of Long Island, since 1639. The Gardiners have preserved the island's forests of white oak, wild cherry, swamp maples, and birch, and protected the wildlife sheltered there.

owned vessels or on one of the ferries that travel between island villages and Long Island towns. On the island, visitors must walk or ride bicycles. Boardwalks serve as streets in most towns. The island's communities cater to a variety of tastes; facilities here range from family-oriented developments to centers of nightlife with an avant-garde clientele.

"What part does the national seashore play on Fire Island?" I asked Joel. He paused for a moment before he replied.

"Fire Island is a tremendous resource," he said, "and we must preserve it. While we respect the rights of communities that were here long before the national seashore was established in 1964, we also welcome visitors and try to provide facilities for them—but in ways that will minimize damage to the environment." Policies intended to protect Fire Island's environment abound. For example, owners of four-wheel-drive vehicles can get permits to drive along the beach at the eastern tip of the island. But only a few year-round residents with special permits are allowed vehicle access to the island's interior.

Despite the presence of public-use facilities on parts of Fire Island, some communities discourage day visitors. Signs at more than one Long Island ferry terminal warn that the island community they serve has no public rest rooms and allows no eating or drinking in public.

"You can't blame those residents too much," a park ranger told me. "Property owners who invest in a beach house to avoid crowds don't

85

Fiery autumn sunset spotlights waterfowl in New Jersey's Brigantine National Wildlife Refuge. Established in 1939 primarily to protect waterfowl along the Atlantic Flyway, where the human population explosion and land development have seriously threatened the birds' existence, Brigantine now encompasses more than 20,000 acres of saltwater and freshwater habitats. Such refuges offer rest and food to waterfowl migrating between arctic waters and warmer waters of the south.

want a flood of day-trippers pouring in." The reason that property owners fear overcrowding became clearer to me when I climbed to the top of the Fire Island Lighthouse. The lighthouse is no longer in use, and the National Park Service plans for the 167-foot-high structure to serve as the focal point of a future museum and visitor center. Ranger Pete Cowan and I trudged up the circular cast-iron stairway, now dusty and speckled with fallen chips of paint.

As we rested at the top, I noticed Pete peering at the skyline. "What are you looking for?" I asked. He pointed to the horizon. "Look there," he said, "you can just make out two tall buildings." There was a bit of haze in the air, but when I looked I could see two tiny towers far in the distance. "Those are the skyscrapers of the World Trade Center in Manhattan," Pete said. "On Fire Island, city life seems far away. It's hard to believe you can actually see buildings in New York City from here without binoculars or a telescope."

It was sobering for me to realize that this tranquil island is only about a three-hour trip from the most populous city in the United States. Thinking of this, I recalled what Joel Pickelner had told me earlier. "Too many visitors would overtax Fire Island, upsetting the delicate balance of its ecology," he had said. "We must respect such limits, for they are imposed not by us but by the island itself."

The islands of New Jersey—the next islands we were to visit—are among the most diverse of our Atlantic isles. As I traveled along the New Jersey coast, I discovered that sometimes I did not know if I was actually on an island. Even with maps, I was at times unsure. A barrier chain stretches for nearly a hundred miles along the coast, from Bay Head near Point Pleasant south to Cape May. Most of this chain is made up of islands, but one part is really a long sand spit—a barrier formation connected at one end to the mainland.

Further complications arise in identifying islands in this region because of the fact that a single storm can breach a spit, thus creating a barrier island overnight. On the other hand, sand deposits can build up until an island becomes connected to the mainland. One place where this has happened is Island Beach State Park. Despite having been an island in the past, this piece of land today is part of a spit.

I sailed to Island Beach with Jeannie and Paul Lucier and Jim McGuire, all of whom I had met as fellow passengers aboard the schooner *Shenandoah* during my travels to Martha's Vineyard. Skilled sailors themselves, they had invited me to visit them when I reached New Jersey. On a bright sunlit morning, the four of us set a course southward from Seaside Park down Barnegat Bay. We were aboard Paul and Jeannie's boat, *Josl,* a 23-foot sailing trimaran, or triple-hulled boat. On our port side lay the barrier strip. Its shore, thoroughly developed this far north, was crowded with vacation homes and other structures. When we reached the state park, its boundary was immediately apparent. Suddenly all traces of human occupation vanished. The shore looked wild, much as it must have appeared centuries ago.

Our destination was the southern tip of Island Beach, where a few summer cottages stand. The cottages were built before the establishment of the park, and their occupants hold lifetime leases. I wanted to talk with one longtime summer resident there, 90-year-old Charlie Burger. Charlie had just put a fish stew on his propane stove when we arrived. All it required was simmering, he insisted as he invited us in.

We talked with Charlie about the forty summers he has spent on Island Beach. He told us that he has seen the shape of the land change considerably. "When this cabin was built," Charlie said, "the inlet was at least half a mile south. It has gradually shifted northward, and now the water's practically lapping at my doorstep. It's just a question of who goes first," Charlie chuckled, "me or the cabin."

A nip of fall was in the air as David Showell and I cast off from the mainland town of Absecon. We were in David's workboat, a wooden-hulled open 14-footer powered by an outboard motor. After serving in the Peace Corps, David—a young man with a neatly trimmed red beard—returned to his coastal New Jersey home to become a waterman. Besides fishing and clamming, he now operates a guide service for fishermen, hunters, and photographers.

David had agreed to take me to the only totally undeveloped barrier island on the New Jersey coast. We wound through channels lined by strands of green cordgrass as we headed northward through Brigantine National Wildlife Refuge on the way to our destination, Little Beach Island. A short distance away, egrets, their feathers gleaming white, stalked their prey or stood as still as sentinels.

When David and I stepped ashore on Little Beach Island, we were the only human beings there. We made *(Continued on page 94)*

Multitude of beachgoers gathers in New York's Jones Beach State Park, where in July 1980 one-

day crowds peaked at 269,000. The park, near New York City, contains seven miles of beaches. 89

*W*ith Manhattan's skyscrapers looming
in the distance, a flock of Canada
geese flies over Jamaica Bay, not far from
Kennedy International Airport (above). At
left, inner-city schoolchildren explore the
Jamaica Bay Unit of Gateway National
Recreation Area with park ranger Jeanette
Parker. Parker instructs children in bird-
watching techniques, using a spotting scope
to locate birds among the tall reed grass
(opposite). Through Gateway, a sprawling
patchwork of land around New York Harbor,
the National Park Service offers city dwellers
the chance to experience nature firsthand.

arrow spit of Sandy Hook (right), site of the nation's oldest original working lighthouse, stretches north from the New Jersey coast. The location of the spit, at the mouth of New York Harbor, once gave it strategic importance for defense fortifications. Sandy Hook has changed repeatedly over the past two centuries, from spit to island and back again. Sand carried by currents has usually rebuilt storm-cut inlets, although on a few occasions, man has had to close the breaches. Below, a sportfisherman casts into the surf for striped bass and bluefish near the Spermaceti Cove Visitor Center. Formerly a station house for the U. S. Life-Saving Service—a forerunner of the U. S. Coast Guard—the center today welcomes visitors to the Sandy Hook Unit of Gateway National Recreation Area.

our way across the island from the bayside to the ocean. At times we followed overgrown paths, and sometimes we struggled through tangled thickets of bayberry. Overhead a marsh hawk suddenly swooped down, dropping like a stone toward unseen prey. Poison ivy grew everywhere.

When we reached the beach, David suggested that I walk along the shore while he cut back across the island to get the boat and bring it around to pick me up. I walked with only sun and sea for company, feeling as alone as Robinson Crusoe before he found Friday's footprints. My mood changed quickly, however, as Brigantine Inlet came into view. There, across a narrow stretch of sparkling water, several fishermen stood on Brigantine Island, their four-wheel-drive vehicles parked on the sand. Even more surprising was the skyline rising in the distance beyond them. Standing alone on this wild, deserted beach, I was looking south at the towering hotels of Atlantic City, on Absecon Island.

In the late 1700s, Absecon Island must have looked much as Little Beach Island does today. Not until 1783 did anyone live on Absecon, and as late as 1850 there were only seven houses on the island. Then in 1852 promoter and civil engineer Richard Osborne planned a railroad line between Philadelphia and the coast, where an island resort would provide much-ballyhooed healthful recreation.

Osborne chose the name Atlantic City for the resort, and he laid out and named its streets. He named many of the north-south avenues for seas and many of the avenues running east and west for states. Today Osborne undoubtedly would be surprised to learn of the fame of some of his street names. Names such as Baltic Avenue and New York Avenue, used in the Monopoly board game, are now familiar to people around the world.

In 1870 the thriving resort town began constructing its famed wooden walkway, the Boardwalk. The walkway was built to help keep sand from being tracked into the lobbies of rooming houses or into the passenger cars of the Camden and Atlantic Railroad. Through the years the Boardwalk continued to be expanded, soon proving a more popular

New high rises line the waterfront of Atlantic City as the former queen of East Coast resorts stages a comeback in the fight for tourist dollars. Founded on Absecon Island in the 1850s as a retreat for Philadelphians, Atlantic City became a national resort by the late 19th century. Spectacular acts drew crowds to the city's amusement piers. Atlantic City declined after air travel made distant locales more accessible. In 1976 the state authorized casino gambling in Atlantic City in an effort to lure visitors.

attraction than the ocean beaches it bordered. By 1902 it had grown to its present dimensions: sixty feet wide and just under four miles long.

Along the Boardwalk, amusement piers jutted into the ocean, offering carnival rides, sideshows, and top entertainers. Souvenir shops, vaudeville theaters, pinball arcades, and the distinctive taste of saltwater taffy also became synonymous with the area. Atlantic City's popularity survived war and depression, but by the 1960s the city's fortunes had declined. "Air travel is what really hurt Atlantic City," a public-relations man there told me. "Why spend a week at the beach here when you can board a plane for Florida or the Bahamas?"

*I*n an attempt to reverse the city's fortunes, the state of New Jersey held a referendum in 1976 that authorized the legalization of casino gambling in Atlantic City. Bringing in gambling was a turnabout for a resort where, until 1940, men who appeared on the beach without bathing tops were subject to arrest.

When Meredith and I arrived in Atlantic City, we checked into Resorts International, the city's first hotel-casino, which opened in May 1978. We were immediately struck by the lack of a casino atmosphere. Far from being the focal point of the hotel complex, the casino is located to one side of the building, away from the majority of traffic. A guest could easily stay at the hotel for weeks and never see a slot machine.

"Atlantic City casinos are planned that way," architect David Jacobson told me over coffee in the conference room of his firm. David, who opened an office in Atlantic City in 1976, has designed several hotel-casinos. "The legislation that authorized casino gambling here was written to preserve Atlantic City's character as a resort and convention center. It is the official policy of the New Jersey Casino Control Commission to prevent the dominance of casinos. To qualify for a casino license, a hotel of at least 500 rooms must be part of the plan. In addition, large amounts of space must be devoted to public areas for restaurants, cabarets, convention halls, or indoor sports facilities."

If the casino was not the focus of our hotel's design, it undoubtedly was the center of attention for its patrons. When Meredith and I first walked through the casino's doors, past the omnipresent security guards, we were impressed by the huge gambling area.

"It's amazing how big they can make it look by using mirrors," Meredith remarked. But as we strolled past banks of gleaming slot machines and long rows of gaming tables, it soon became evident that the room's vastness was not the result of illusion.

"Our casino is about the size of two football fields," Director of Public Relations Philip Wechsler told me. "We have 123 gaming tables, and well over 1,600 slot machines."

"How much money do people spend here?" I asked.

"So far in 1981, the casino's winnings have averaged $590,000 a day," he replied. "On our biggest day, which was July 4, the casino made $1,349,100. Don't forget, though, that we don't get to keep all that money. In 1980 we paid $34,000,000 to the state of New Jersey in gaming taxes alone."

What kind of people were filling the casino's coffers to overflowing? Certainly not the high rollers in flashy suits or the legendary little old ladies in tennis shoes I half expected to find. At every casino I visited, the patrons looked like people you might expect to find in shopping centers.

South of Absecon Island, I visited Seven Mile Beach, an island with two small summer resort towns, Avalon and Stone Harbor. I was fascinated here by the contrasting ways the members of this island's two communities have chosen to protect their properties.

"I've lived here in Avalon for 16 years, and I've served as mayor since 1973," Ellsworth Armacost told me when I visited him in his office. "I think I can speak for our whole town when I say that we're really proud of our beaches and dunes, and we're committed to preserving them. Without the protection of the dunes, we'd be vulnerable to every storm that came along."

He was referring to the dune line established between the town and its broad beach. Unlike many other coastal communities I visited, Avalon has chosen to work with the natural processes of a barrier island, not to fight against them.

"We try to make maintaining the dunes a matter of civic pride," Mayor Armacost told me. "Every year Avalon's schoolchildren join in a program of planting beach grass on the dunes. In this way, not only do they help to maintain a valuable resource, but they also learn about the ecosystem of the dunes and the importance of preserving them."

Along with a friend of mine, Joe Lomax, a longtime resident of southern New Jersey who is an environmental consultant and a nature photographer, I walked a narrow, carefully marked pathway over the dunes to the beach at Avalon. Behind the dunes grew a thicket of bayberry, juniper, and wild cherry trees, liberally interspersed with poison ivy. At the crest of the dunes we paused, and Joe pointed to the beach grass growing there. "Although these plants are tough enough to withstand salt spray and pounding storm waves," he remarked, "they cannot survive trampling. That is why it is so important to keep people off the dunes. Without plants to stabilize the sand, it quickly blows away."

A few miles south, at Stone Harbor Point, there were no dunes to cross. Instead, Joe and I climbed over a heavy timber retaining wall faced with a reinforced concrete-and-rock abutment.

"This looks strong enough to last forever," I commented.

"It does here," Joe replied. "But let's go look at what's happening down at the south end of the beach." I was surprised at what I saw there. Behind the seemingly impregnable retaining wall, erosion had set in. Huge horizontal timbers that had once anchored the wall in the earth now lay fully exposed. That shocked me. But what was amazing was the speed at which erosion has taken place here. "I estimate that this summer alone we've lost more than twenty feet of beach to erosion," Joe said. "Compared with this, the beach at Avalon is far more stable.

"But don't be too hasty in contrasting these communities," Joe added quickly. "It's not simply a matter of environmental concern. After all, within Stone Harbor's city limits is a municipal bird sanctuary where a third of the state's population of herons, egrets, and glossy ibises comes to nest every summer. Rather, it's the choice each community has made about how to protect itself: by attempting to defy the natural processes of a barrier island, or by cooperating with them. Here on a single island, you can see how well both ways are working."

This same problem of which approach to use in protecting beaches exists in other areas. "There are 48 ocean-front municipalities along the coast of New Jersey," Dr. David N. Kinsey told me in his office in Trenton, the state capital. Dr. Kinsey is the Director of the Division of

Coastal Resources for the New Jersey Department of Environmental Protection. "Many of these municipalities were built before scientists became aware of how barrier islands serve to protect the mainland from the effects of storms and high tides.

"Consequently, you'll see places where the dunes have been bull-dozed flat to make building lots. That's when the problems began. Beaches eroded away in those areas. Seawalls and other protective structures were then constructed to prevent further erosion and storm damage. But these structures have been expensive to build and largely ineffective over the years.

Surrounded by Victorian gilt and glitter, gamblers in the Golden Nugget Casino go for the elusive jackpot. Decorated in the opulent style of Atlantic City's

19th-century heyday, the 40,800-square-foot casino offers patrons slot machines, roulette, and several card and dice games. On an average day the casino grosses more than $400,000, of which 8 percent in taxes goes toward senior citizen programs. Since 1976, investors have spent 1.5 billion dollars building hotel-casinos in Atlantic City.

"Obviously, we can't immediately undo damage that has been taking place for generations. And we have to consider the impact of any changes we propose on property owners, people who have made investments in homes and businesses along the coast. But we've made a start in dealing with these problems," Dr. Kinsey said, handing me an inch-and-a-half-thick book weighing about four pounds. "This is a draft of a shore protection plan for the entire New Jersey coast," he said. "It's bold and innovative, and it's the first time we've ever proposed anything like it.

"But no plan, however good, can succeed without public support," Dr. Kinsey concluded. "Basically, what we have to do is to begin changing people's perceptions. People must realize that they need to begin working with nature, not against it."

Listening to Dr. Kinsey, I wished for more time to explore and to learn about our Atlantic islands. But for now my travels were to end in southern New Jersey. My colleague Chris Lee, however, was to visit many other islands to the south, including some that have been virtually unaltered by humans. Chris would see such places as she began her travels in the Virginia barrier islands.

*W*hite feathers tinged red by the fading sunset, snow geese flutter above a tidal marsh at Brigantine National Wildlife Refuge, only a few miles from downtown Atlantic City. Marsh grasses supply ample food for as many as 60,000 snow geese that stop at Brigantine in November and December during their annual migration south. At first freeze, most will move on to the Chesapeake or Delaware Bay regions. From nature trails, observation towers, and an eight-mile auto route, visitors at Brigantine can observe great concentrations of geese, ducks, shorebirds, and warblers. At right, a great blue heron, its long neck folded between its shoulders, rests on an ice-encrusted bank. These solitary wading birds stand motionless as they wait to catch fish, frogs, snakes, crustaceans, small mammals, or insects to eat.

Pounded by early morning breakers, a pier at Nags Head, in North Carolina's Outer Banks,

Against the Sea

By Christine Eckstrom Lee

awaits the daily tide of fishermen. Anglers here cast for king mackerel, blues, and other fish.

*T*hose who knew Hog Island called it paradise. It was "a place for free spirits," one islander said of this sandy strip of land off Virginia's Eastern Shore. A 1903 news story described the island as "nestling in the bosom of old ocean like a gem." More than 400 people once lived in the town of Broadwater, at the southern tip of Hog Island. They fished and hunted, and their homes were shaded by a tall pine forest.

"Welcome to Broadwater," Barry Truitt said to me as we stood on Hog Island. Arms outstretched, he faced the open Atlantic, whose waves were splashing around my feet. "Most of what used to be Broadwater is out there now, under the deep blue sea."

I looked around. There were no people, no homes, no pines. Only a rolling prairie of low, grassy dunes stretched across Hog Island, from the beach to the inland coastal salt marsh. Nothing suggested that Broadwater had ever existed.

Like most of the islands along Virginia's Eastern Shore, Hog Island is not widely known. Few maps show small islands such as Hog, one of 18 Virginia barrier isles. Maps of Virginia on coffeehouse place mats sometimes even fail to include the state's Eastern Shore, a 75-mile-long finger of land separating the Chesapeake Bay from the Atlantic Ocean. However, in a nation where some fifty million people live within fifty miles of the Atlantic Coast and where thousands of people have cottages on what were once deserted beaches, this very lack of fame may have helped preserve the beauty of Hog Island, the first place I visited in my travels. Like my colleague Bob Morrison, I was to visit dozens of islands, beginning here in Virginia's barrier isles and ending in the Florida Keys.

Hog Island is part of a sanctuary now, and Barry Truitt works to protect it. More than 90 percent of the island is included in the Virginia Coast Reserve. This sanctuary was set aside in the early 1970s by the Nature Conservancy, a private conservation organization that owns all or part of 13 islands fringing Virginia's Eastern Shore. Encompassing nearly 35,000 acres of islands and marshes, the reserve extends along 51 miles of seacoast. The faces of the islands present a variety of expressions: Parramore has white dunes and a forest of eighty-foot-tall pines; Smith is ribbed with thickets and freshwater swales; Godwin's marshes are braided with serpentine channels.

The reserve is a living laboratory for barrier island research. More than 200 species of birds rest, nest, or live on the islands, and 90 percent of the finfish and shellfish harvested on the Eastern Shore begin life in the lush salt marshes sheltered behind the islands. Loggerhead turtles, a threatened species, emerge from the sea to bury their eggs on the islands' beaches, and some small mammals that inhabit the scrub thickets and the maritime forests have evolved unique features in island isolation: A cottontail found on one island has been classed as a distinct subspecies.

On a sunny June day I motored across the shallows between the mainland and Hog Island with Barry, assistant manager of the Virginia Coast Reserve. Tall and black-bearded, he looks more like a lumberjack than a marine biologist. A patch on his visor shows a fish breaking the water, revealing his favorite sport. Barry holds the Virginia state tarpon record for a 130-pounder he landed off the barrier islands.

"Barrier islands such as Hog are actually waves of sand," Barry explained as we walked along the beach. The sand was hot and crunchy underfoot with the shells of whelks, clams, and scallops. "If you come out here during a storm, you'll see tons of sand blowing down the beach

Buffer zone for the nation's midsection: Barrier spits and islands shield the mainland from the wrath of the Atlantic Ocean. As fluid as desert dunes, these narrow strips of sand change constantly—waxing, waning, and migrating while the sea washes sand away here and piles it there. Resorts line some barrier beaches, but many islands remain wild.

NORTH CAROLINA

Wilmington •

S. C.

MAP ART BY SUZANNE BURTON

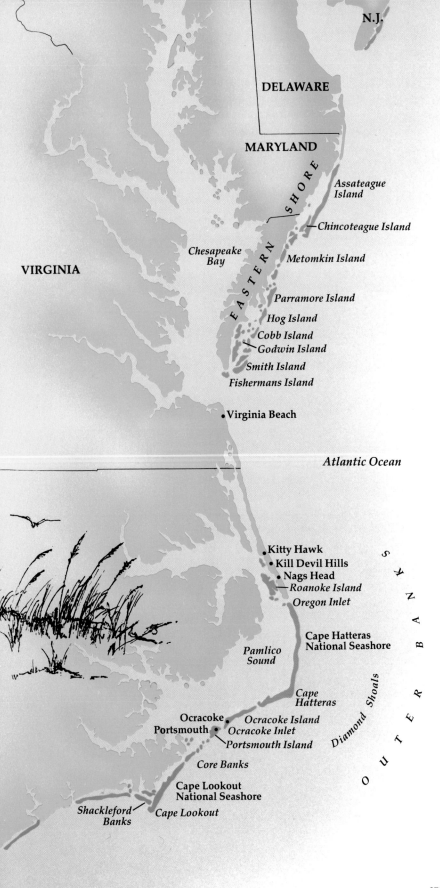

N.J.

DELAWARE

MARYLAND

E A S T E R N   S H O R E

Assateague Island

Chincoteague Island

Chesapeake Bay

VIRGINIA

Metomkin Island

Parramore Island

Hog Island

Cobb Island

Godwin Island

Smith Island

Fishermans Island

•Virginia Beach

Atlantic Ocean

•Kitty Hawk

•Kill Devil Hills

•Nags Head

—*Roanoke Island*

Oregon Inlet

Cape Hatteras
National Seashore

Pamlico Sound

Cape Hatteras

O U T E R   B A N K S

Diamond Shoals

Ocracoke
Portsmouth•

Ocracoke Island

Ocracoke Inlet

Portsmouth Island

Core Banks

Cape Lookout
National Seashore

Shackleford Banks

Cape Lookout

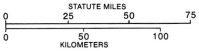

STATUTE MILES

0   25   50   75

0   50   100

KILOMETERS

every minute. The grasses catch the sand and build dunes, protecting the rest of the island. But the most important thing about barrier islands is that the wind and the ocean move them around. Now if you owned a house on this beach you would say, 'The island is washing away!' It's not. The island is migrating, that's all. These islands are moving around, just the way they always have."

Near the site of Broadwater, Barry crouched to draw a map in the sand. "Migration is what happened here, too," he said. "A hundred years ago, Hog Island was shaped like a long, thin teardrop. Broadwater was on the southern, wider, end of the island. Today the island's shape is almost the reverse." He sketched another teardrop over the first, with the thin part of the drop now at the bottom. "The beach on the southern end of the island is more than a mile and a half west of where it was a century ago." As Barry spoke, the warm breeze that rippled our shirts slowly filled the grooves of his map with sand.

The people of Broadwater knew their island was moving. But, until the 1930s, few chose to leave their homes in Hog Island's pine woods. The sea washed closer. After a severe storm flooded the town in 1933, many residents floated their homes to the mainland by barge. More storms struck, and finally the last islanders moved away. Today watermen report seeing gravestones in the shallows off Hog Island. The forest is gone; Broadwater is gone. Where townspeople once picnicked in the shade of pines, dolphins now leap, channel bass run, and whelks inch along the sandy bottom.

In the epic of barrier island dramas, the story of Broadwater is only one stanza. Change is a constant throughout the long string of barrier islands that lace the U. S. shoreline from New England to the Gulf Coast of Texas. Barrier island land has never been stable; tales abound of islands popping up and down, growing fat or thin, and shifting to a different position. Most geologists believe that the barrier islands were formed after the last Ice Age glacier receded about 15,000 years ago. At that time, glacial ice held huge amounts of the earth's water; sea level was hundreds of feet lower; and the East Coast shoreline was many miles farther out, at the edge of the continental shelf. As the ice melted, rivers carried sand to the coast. The sea level rose, and waves pushed more sand to the beaches. The wind sculpted the sand into dunes. The oceans rose higher and broke through the wall of dunes at many points, flooding the lowlands behind the dunes and creating the barrier islands.

The islands are still moving because the sea level is still rising, though the rate of rise has fluctuated over the years. Until about 5,000 years ago the sea was rising roughly three feet each century. Many geologists believe it is now rising at a rate of about a foot per century. As long as the sea creeps higher, the islands will continue to move.

"*T*his is the least altered set of natural barrier islands on the Atlantic and Gulf Coasts of the United States," said Rod Hennessey, a young wildlife ecologist and manager of the Virginia Coast Reserve. We sat on a creekside dock at Brownsville, an early 19th-century plantation on the Eastern Shore that is being restored as a headquarters for the reserve. "We're trying to protect the natural diversity represented in these islands. So many environments are disappearing faster than we can understand them. In the future, when someone wants to see how a natural barrier island system works, these islands will be here."

The shadow of a magnificent creature passing over the marshes and dunes of the Virginia barrier islands is testimony to the diversity of the land. Ornithologists at Cornell University selected the islands as a site for reintroducing a bird that has all but vanished from the eastern United States: the peregrine falcon, one of the world's swiftest birds.

"The peregrine is an environmental barometer," Rod explained. "The birds are at the tip of the food pyramid. Contaminants concentrate at each step up the food chain, which makes the falcons terribly susceptible. We knew the peregrines were disappearing and that something must be wrong." What was wrong was DDT. This pesticide caused peregrines to lay eggs with thin shells. Brooding mothers crushed their own eggs. The entire eastern peregrine population was gone by the 1960s. Then scientists at Cornell began a project to raise peregrines in captivity. In 1975 the first falcons were released at five eastern sites, and in 1980 four chicks were born in the wild—the first in twenty years.

Several days after my visit with Rod Hennessey, I stood on the roof of an old Coast Guard station at the southern tip of Cobb Island, in the Virginia Coast Reserve. In the distance a falcon soared in from the north, landing on a platform mounted on a tower above the surrounding marsh. Four other peregrines on the platform watched him arrive, and I watched them all through binoculars. (Continued on page 114)

Young Louisiana heron stands lookout atop a bush on Metomkin Island, one of 18 Virginia barrier islands. Metomkin and all or part of 12 other islands make up the Virginia Coast Reserve, a wildlife sanctuary privately owned by the Nature Conservancy. The reserve's beaches, woods, and salt marshes support a varied population that includes white-tailed deer, otters, mink, cormorants, and loons, as well as such rarities as peregrine falcons and loggerhead turtles.

Saltwater cowboys ride herd on Assateague Island's best-known residents: its wild ponies (above). Well adapted to their marshy environment off the coast of Maryland and Virginia, these compact, shaggy horses have tolerated the island's brackish water, salt hay, green-headed flies, and winter winds since before the Revolutionary War. Legends trace their ancestry to pirates' mounts or to survivors from the holds of shipwrecked galleons. More recent arrivals include mustangs (left) imported from Utah and Nevada in the

1970s to rejuvenate bands decimated by swamp fever. Today two groups roam Assateague's wilderness: the 40-head "Maryland herd" owned by the National Park Service and the 150-head "Virginia herd" belonging to the Volunteer Fire Company of nearby Chincoteague Island. Each July Chincoteague firemen trade rubber boots and slickers for quarter horses and western wear (right). The firemen-turned-cowboys round up the wild ponies for health checkups. They then swim the herd across a hundred-yard channel to Chincoteague, where they auction off about forty foals and yearlings. The annual sale ensures a stable equine population and provides Chincoteaguers with funds to equip their fire department.

*C*orralled by the waters of Assateague
Channel, ponies swim to market.
Thousands of tourists delight in the
annual event, traditionally followed by a parade
down Chincoteague's Main Street. At the
city's carnival grounds, visitors can view the
horses, eat "Pony Tail Taffy," and reminisce
over Misty of Chincoteague—a book that
immortalized the island and its ponies.

Center of attention:
Visitors young and old gather
to pet a colt displayed
before the Chincoteague
auction. Small, hardy,
and easily trained to the
saddle, the ponies sold here
make excellent mounts for
children. Such ponies usually
go for $200 to $500, but
prices vary widely. The
favorite of 1980 drew a
record $1,250 bid.

Armada of royal terns fills the evening sky as parents bring minnows to their earthbound

chicks on Virginia's Fishermans Island, site of a thousand-acre national wildlife refuge.

*C*hicken-wire stockade encloses one morning's catch
of royal tern chicks herded from among the dunes on
Metomkin Island, Virginia. The catch included a
few sandwich terns, which often share nesting sites with
royal terns. Author Chris Lee, foreground, passes chicks
for banding to Karen Mayne of the U. S. Fish and Wildlife
Service and Smithsonian Institution Research Associate
Dr. John Weske. They then attach a metal leg band to each
youngster (opposite, top) before releasing it. The caged
fledglings (left) instinctively mass together.

"We're baby-sitting," explained Hans Gabler, a graduate student at the College of William and Mary. Using an adaptation of the falconer's training technique known as hacking, Hans and co-worker Randy Downer were caring for the 2-month-old peregrines until they learned to fly free and to hunt on their own.

Cages of quail filled a garage adjoining the station. When the falcons fly off to explore, Hans or Randy slips out to the tower and leaves them quail. "It's a strange situation," said Hans. "They can never know that we're feeding them or they would fly to us and beg. It is possible to tame a peregrine, but a tame falcon would probably be shot.

"Working here, we've watched them learn to fly. They take off from the tower and circle straight up and out of sight. After they eat they go for evening flights and practice chasing ocean birds. Seeing their progress day after day, I really want to be closer to them, but I realize that would likely be their death sentence."

Beachcombers heed the elemental symphony of the sea on a deserted beach close to Nags Head. Nags Head lies near the northern end of the Outer Banks, a region that includes both Cape Hatteras and Cape Lookout National Seashores.

The peregrines grouped together on their covered platform, stretching their wings and glancing over the landscape with eyes like dark marbles. Below them, green marshes spread north to the horizon. Blue creeks looped through the marshes behind the low dunes. To the east, the surf traced a thin white line along the beach.

By midsummer the falcons would be on their own. If reintroduction succeeds, the peregrines will nest in the tower when they mature. If their young survive, peregrine falcons may again be seen sailing on airstreams above the islands and diving at 175-mile-an-hour speeds, restoring a majestic creature to the skies.

Islands of nesting birds sprinkled Metomkin Island, northernmost of the Virginia Coast Reserve isles, the day I visited there to help band a colony of young royal terns. "This will be sort of like a cattle roundup," explained Dr. John Weske as we arrived on Metomkin. Dr. Weske is a research associate at the Smithsonian Institution. For more than ten years he has studied royal terns and other birds that nest in colonies, from the Maryland and Virginia barrier islands to southern North Carolina. His research is focused on the distribution patterns of royal terns, and a key part of his work involves banding young chicks each year. Dr. Weske's enthusiasm for banding birds prompts him to carry eight or ten different sizes of bands whenever he travels to the coast.

It was just after dawn when we arrived. Working with a group of experienced volunteers from the Nature Conservancy and the U. S. Fish and Wildlife Service, we set up a huge circular pen of wire mesh between the surf and the dunes. A wall of wire fanned out from each side of the opening, forming a corridor leading into the ring. We tied carpenter's aprons around our waists, filled the pockets with metal bands, and spaced ourselves in a line across the dunes. Then the drive began.

Marching together in slow, even steps, we waved our arms. Suddenly royal tern chicks began to appear. They ran out from the beach grasses, peeping and pumping their downy wings, not yet able to fly. Thousands of parents filled the sky above us with a dissonant chorus of screams. Hundreds more of the chicks scurried out, like animals fleeing a brush fire. Up the beach at the edge of the dunes, Dr. Weske stood at the northern boundary of the colony. As the chicks approached him, they turned to the beach as if deflected by an invisible wall, angled south, and ran in a waddling, cheeping, fluffy white mass toward the pen.

There were more than 1,600 chicks. We surrounded them, guided them into the pen, and settled down to more than two hours of banding. An open metal band was slipped onto each chick's leg and squeezed shut with pliers. Then the chick was released to run back up the beach into the dunes, where it would be quickly reunited with its parents.

"Royal tern colonies are extremely vulnerable," Dr. Weske explained. "The birds nest in dense aggregations, a beak's reach apart. And they nest in very few places, so that a disaster in one colony can have a profound impact on the population." Birds that nest in colonies or on beaches are highly susceptible to changes in their habitat and to disturbances by man. More than 25 species of such birds nest in the Virginia barrier islands, a shorebird's arcadia.

*T*he islands along the Atlantic shore are more than a haven for wildlife. To the first Europeans reaching the continent, the coast and the nearby islands were the American frontier, and the early settlements were there: Plymouth, Port Royal, St. Augustine. In 1585 the first English colonists to establish a foothold in North America arrived on Roanoke Island, in what is now North Carolina's Outer Banks. A second major colony arrived in 1587. Within three years, these settlers had mysteriously vanished. The group later became known as the "Lost Colony." But the tide of immigration into this area had begun. Today some Outer Banks residents live in villages established by their ancestors before the Founding Fathers penned the Constitution.

A startling photograph of eastern North Carolina taken from space by Apollo astronauts reveals the Outer Banks as a thread of sandy isles between the dark Atlantic and the pale shallows of Pamlico Sound. Extending from the Virginia border south to Cape Lookout, the 180-mile-long barrier chain bends like an arm to shelter inland marshes and lowlands. Midway down the Outer Banks, the elbow of Cape Hatteras juts out to sea. Waves sweeping along the Cape carry sand that is deposited offshore, forming treacherous Diamond Shoals. The stormy waters in this area, where countless vessels have been lost, are known to mariners as the "Graveyard of the Atlantic."

My first view of the Outer Banks, as I drove south along the road from Kitty Hawk, was of a land as spare as a skeleton. The works of man seemed to stand in defiance of the elements. Houses were perched atop pilings twice the height of the buildings themselves. The road seemed to run barely above sea level, and at times I could look left to the Atlantic and right to the sound as I cruised along a strip of sand only a few hundred yards wide.

*T*he northern section of the Outer Banks, from the North Carolina state line to Oregon Inlet, is technically not an island but a barrier spit attached to the mainland south of Virginia Beach. Later, when I flew over the Outer Banks, I mentioned this to pilot Jay Mankedick of Kitty Hawk. He laughed, "Three small children with toy shovels could make it an island in one day."

Nags Head is the hub of the northern Banks. One of the earliest Atlantic beach resorts, the town has thrived since the 1830s. The first cottages and hotels for summer guests rose on the soundside near the homes of Banker fishermen. A century later, the town had spread to the sea, and a mile-long row of rustic cottages lined the beach. Nags Head's popularity blossomed after bridges from the mainland and highways down the island were completed in the 1930s. Motels, homes, campgrounds, and businesses now stretch north and south of the core community along 75 miles of oceanfront. Signs along the main strip read like a fast-food anthology, and flashing neon announces Nags Head's varied offerings.

Between Nags Head and Kitty Hawk lies the town of Kill Devil Hills. This area was a desolate expanse in 1900 when an Ohio man wrote of his plans to visit the Outer Banks ". . . for the purpose of making some experiments with a flying machine." On December 17, 1903, Orville Wright and his brother, Wilbur, made the first successful powered airplane flight above the rolling dunes of Kill Devil Hills.

Five miles south of the site of that first flight stands 140-foot-high Jockey Ridge, the largest sand dune on the U. S. Atlantic Coast. Late on a hot summer afternoon I ran off a sand cliff below Jockey Ridge and flew, in my own jubilant tribute to the Wright Brothers. I was in a hang glider, and instructor Randy Cobb of Kitty Hawk Kites had just explained the procedures for my first flight. But nothing he said prepared me for the sensation of flying.

As I ran to the edge of the dune, the wind lifted me before I could take my last step, and I soared. Every effort of my body, all the will of my mind, was concentrated on the goal of never touching down, on the desire to fly forever. I suppose my first glide was briefer than the Wright Brothers' 12-second flight. That matters little; I have it to remember, and my suspicions are confirmed that eagles and falcons and hawks sailing the unseen currents of the skies are sometimes soaring for pure joy.

At Whalebone Junction, below Nags Head, the visual character of

Besieged beacon for the "Graveyard of the Atlantic," 110-year-old Cape Hatteras Lighthouse stands in danger of collapse. In the last century, the turbulent surf, coupled with the rising sea level, has erased more than 2,000 feet of land that once separated the lighthouse from the water. Today the beacon sits only about a hundred feet from the sea. Ideas for saving this National Historic Landmark—the emblem of Cape Hatteras National Seashore and, at 208 feet, the tallest lighthouse in the United States—include moving the 2,600-ton sentinel inland, buttressing its base with sand and concrete, and anchoring plastic seaweed offshore to defuse the ocean's power and hold the sand in place.

the region changes. Visitors who follow the highway south soon enter the other world of the Outer Banks—the Cape Hatteras National Seashore. With the exception of eight villages, the area from Whalebone Junction to the southern tip of Ocracoke Island is a 72-mile-long continuum of surf, dunes, marsh, and shallows. Set aside in 1953, the park was our first national seashore. Although millions of beachcombers, surf fishermen, and bird-watchers visit Hatteras each year, there is always an empty stretch of sand to be found. At the peak of the summer season, when the breezes at Nags Head carry Top 40 tunes and the scent of coconut oil, I could walk the beaches of Hatteras and see only dolphins.

No bridges lead to Ocracoke. It is an island in the truest sense of the word. A ferry from the tip of Hatteras Island transports passengers and vehicles across the inlet to Ocracoke, and a 13-mile-long road between grassy dunes and thick hammocks leads to Ocracoke Village. Sheltered by live oaks, loblollies, and cedars at the southwest corner of the island, the village centers on a round harbor known as Silver Lake. Across the wide shallows of Ocracoke Inlet lies the island of Portsmouth.

The opening or closing of inlets has changed the number and size of Outer Banks islands throughout history, but since the time of the Roanoke colonists the inlet between (Continued on page 126)

*O*ceanfront homes crowd perilously near the surf at Nags Head. The beach here shrinks steadily as the sea encroaches. Early residents of barrier islands shunned such locations, choosing sites inland or on the sheltered baysides. During this century, however, coastal construction boomed, fueled by the desire to live at water's edge—and by government subsidies for access roads, low-cost flood insurance, beach restoration, and shoreline maintenance. Today ecologists know that despite man's best efforts the world's rising sea level will continue to make barrier islands migrate toward the mainland, seaward edges eroding as bayside shores increase. The sensible approach, according to the ecologists:

discourage outer beach development, stop trying to hold back the sea, and let nature take its course. Also under attack: the greatly increased use of ORVs—off-road vehicles—on fragile barrier islands *(above)*. Such vehicles can quickly destroy beach grasses. As a result, the dunes erode more rapidly.

Scalloped shores, oak-shaded streets, and a colorful past embrace Ocracoke Island, landfall for

Sir Walter Raleigh's colonists in 1585 and 18th-century port for Blackbeard and other pirates.

*C*lam rakes churning the shallows, Sue Harvey, the wife of photographer Dave Harvey, and sons Erin, center, and Bryan, right, harvest the hard-shelled bounty of Ocracoke Inlet in an area called Teach's Hole. Named for Edward Teach—Blackbeard—who met his end here at the hands of British mariners in 1718, the channel provides a year-round clamming and fishing spot. The Harveys use a favorite Ocracoke ploy: Their cooler, mounted aboard an inner tube and lashed to the waist lest changing tides set it adrift, provides a mobile storage compartment for clams. Afternoon brings a full cooler and an old-fashioned clambake on one of Ocracoke's wide beaches (below), where a potluck dinner features the day's take grilled over an open fire (opposite, bottom). The party includes several islanders and summer residents.

Blustery sky highlights a dune in the making: Fringe of salt-tolerant sea oats captures

windblown sand and gradually overgrows it, anchoring once-loose grains into a dune ridge.

Portsmouth and Ocracoke has remained open. In the mid-18th century, communities of merchants and ships' pilots were established on each side of Ocracoke Inlet. The seamen guided vessels and unloaded cargo for transport to the mainland. Many of Ocracoke's more than 650 current residents are descended from the original settlers of what was then called Pilot Town. One resident, Myra Wahab, lives in a house facing Silver Lake that is shaded by live oaks and framed by a picket fence.

Myra told me that her late husband, Stanley, traced his ancestry to the 1700s, when a shipwrecked sailor named Wahab was cast ashore on the island. Her own family began visiting Ocracoke before the turn of the century, when travelers arrived in steamers and sailing ships and a tram line drawn by horses carried hotel guests to the beach. With time came paved roads and automobiles, the national seashore and more visitors, and fierce storms from the sea that reshaped the land.

But change has brushed the village with a soft hand. On Myra's wall is a faded photograph of Ocracoke taken from the top of the town's whitewashed lighthouse in 1904. "You see, it looks much the same," she said. "All of those homes are still here. Ocracoke has a stable population. Some of the children may have to leave to make a living, but many will return. They always have." Myra's face is animated and full of smiles, and she sits tall on the edge of her chair at the mention of fishing. "Everybody here goes fishing," she said, "and I'll surf fish up until mid-November barefooted."

Myra offered me fresh figs from her yard and showed me her yaupon tree, whose leaves were used by Indians and early settlers to make a purgative tea. "Islands make their people self-sufficient," she said, "and you have to make your own fun. But if someone runs into trouble, everybody helps out. I've had people say to me, 'Why in the world do you want to live on Ocracoke? There's nothing to do.' There's more to do here than I can possibly accomplish, and I just plain love every inch of it."

If each place has an essence that waits for discovery by those who would learn the land, then the essence of Ocracoke is peace. Summer days are sunny and sultry here, and the shady sand lanes that wind through the village are soft against the soles of bare feet. I was drawn to the rhythms of life around the harbor: Ferries leaving for the mainland

Weathered relic from an age of heroes, 70-year-old Chicamacomico Lifesaving Station, on Hatteras Island, recalls days when the U. S. Life-Saving Service kept men and surfboats constantly at the ready to assist shipwrecked crews. Abandoned in 1954 and now owned in part by the Chicamacomico Historical Association, the station today awaits restoration.

sound deep horns; people gather at the post office for mail and news; fishing boats return with sea bass and shrimp; and the Ocracoke lighthouse shines at dusk. Beyond the embracing circle of life in the village lies the wild release of the sea. On hot afternoons I walked across the grassy flats to dive into the blue-and-white waves. Reaching the top of the dunes and seeing the ocean, I felt as if I had found a favorite thing I had hidden long ago.

No homes line the dunes of Ocracoke. "The traditional residents of these islands knew where to build their houses," explained Dave Frum, a young West Virginian who has served as the National Park Service interpreter on Ocracoke for three years. "The village was built on the widest part of the island, away from the ocean. People weren't looking for a surfside view; they were here to make a living, and they knew the sea."

We walked along the beach flats at the southern end of Ocracoke. "The Park Service has experimented through the years with building dunes along the seashore, trying to stop the ocean. We realize now that it really doesn't work, and the new strategy is to let nature take its course, to let the barrier islands revert to a natural condition." In the distance, the waters of Ocracoke Inlet peaked white on the shoals.

"People with homes on the beach are gambling against the odds," said Dave. "They just don't understand the power of that ocean. So many of us come here when the water is nice and calm, and we can't imagine what it can do. Sometimes I look at the ocean in the winter and I think, 'I'd better get away from here.' But very few islanders leave during storms. One man told me last year, 'Where else am I supposed to go? All my family is here. Everything I own is here. I'll ride it out.'"

*L*ike the residents of Ocracoke, the people of Portsmouth knew the fury of the sea. Now being restored as a historic site, Portsmouth marks the northern boundary of the Cape Lookout National Seashore. Extending south for 55 miles along Core and Shackleford Banks, the seashore is wild and unpopulated, and Portsmouth Village crowns the barren beaches of the Banks like a green oasis.

Located at the northern end of the island, Portsmouth Village was founded in 1753. Like its sister town of Ocracoke across the inlet, Portsmouth was settled by merchants and pilots. For more than a century, the village thrived. With 500 residents, it was once the largest town on the Banks. Then slowly, steadily, over the past century the population dwindled. Storms battered the island. Shoals formed in the inlet, and Portsmouth lost the maritime traffic it needed to survive. With reluctance, Portsmouth families moved away. In 1971 the last two permanent residents left the island.

A storm was approaching as I stood on Portsmouth Island. From the horizon to the shallows, gray seas rocked. The wind spun spray from the breakers and swept sheets of sand down the beach. Low clouds raced across the island. Westward, over the dunes and flats, grasses bowed and shook. Gulls soared overhead, sounding cries that the wind tore from their open bills. As the gusts reached the line of thickets and trees that shelter Portsmouth Village, myrtles, pines, and cedars caught the wind.

At the white clapboard church in the heart of the village, people were filing inside for a special Sunday service. The church was full as the Reverend Jimmy Creech of Ocracoke stood before the congregation, waiting for the last few members to arrive. Past residents, families, and friends had gathered on Portsmouth Island this day for a homecoming. Inside the church, people talked, embraced, nodded greetings. Some clasped ridged hands and strained to see the friend hidden beneath the changes age had made. Many eyes moved from face to face along the pews, and many eyes held tears.

As the last man was seated at the end of my pew, the woman behind him leaned forward and spoke softly, "Ben Salter!" He turned around slowly and smiled. "How are you?" she said. "It's Margaret, Margaret McWilliams Smith. It's been nearly seventy years since I've been back." His eyes brimmed. "Margaret!" The service began, and the members of the congregation bowed their heads in prayer.

"We have not been lost, but we have returned home," Mr. Creech told the congregation. "The place that we call home is more than just the location of our birth. It gives us the images by which we understand ourselves and our world. An island is not just sand that sits in a body of water. It is a land in union with the seas around it." After the service, the rains began to fall, and the wind and the breakers sculpted new forms in the sands of Portsmouth Island.

North of the Cape Lookout lighthouse, I crossed Core Banks from the salt marsh to the beach with Dr. Orrin Pilkey, a marine geologist from Duke University. We were searching for clues to where this island had been. Just as every criminal leaves a bit of evidence behind, an island leaves a bread-crumb trail of its past. Our search was a journey through Holocene times, the recent geologic period from about 7,000 years ago to the present. I had always thought of changes in the earth as infinitely slow processes spanning unimaginable periods of time. In the case of island migration, a geologic event was happening before my eyes.

"This is a genuine overwash fan," said Orrin, with the pleasure of a painter unveiling his masterpiece. We stood on a flat sand plain dotted with green shoots on the inland side of the island. "Storm waves carry sand from the beach to the soundside, where fresh spartina grass takes root. We're standing on a future salt marsh." We waded through waist-high spartina grass fringing the shore. "In order to be happy, this grass has to be flooded daily," he explained. "New marsh acts as a baffle, trapping sediments and gradually building up into genuine land. Eventually, where we are right now will be the middle of the island."

We hiked into the dunes. "As rising sea level and storms push the beaches back, sand is washed over the island. The fan becomes marsh, the marsh becomes new land, and the island has rolled over itself and moved toward the mainland. Twenty years ago we didn't know all these things," he added. "We were basically in the dark about beaches."

Orrin Pilkey is a geological activist, and his enthusiasm is infectious. "I spend a lot of time trying to bridge the gap between beach scientists and the public," he explained. Orrin makes long trips from his home in Durham, North Carolina, to appear at town meetings along the coast. Often, he raises the sole voice of dissent against what he sees as unsafe shoreline planning. "I hadn't even seen the ocean until after graduate school," Orrin told me. He studied geology at Washington State University and received his master's degree from the University of Montana. He moved to Florida to do his doctoral work. "That's where I got into marine science," he said. "First I studied the beaches, then

Beach grasses top a dune crest on Ocracoke Island. Established dune ridges such as this help absorb the sea's energy and protect the maritime forests behind the dunes. The ridges may be quite narrow or extend back from the beach for several hundred feet.

I moved to the continental shelf, and now I've gone to the deep sea. I'm going steadily outward and down. That's where it all begins."

As we walked toward the surf, I told him about patches of marsh I had seen on the Virginia barrier island beaches. "That's a big clue," he said. "Those islands are really moving fast." He picked up a marsh snail. "We found this same species in sand 16,000 feet down, 150 miles off-shore. When the sea was lower, there was a marsh, like this one, on the continental shelf. When the sea rose, the sediments slid down the slope and were deposited on the ocean floor. We were really excited to find that sediment because it confirmed our ideas about island movement."

Another clue. Orrin pointed out the brown stains on the seashells along the beach. "That color is due to iron oxides, and the interesting thing to geologists is that the brown staining occurs only on beaches. So when I find brown-stained shells in my samples offshore, I know that I've struck an old beach."

He scooped up a handful of black sand. "Compare this sand with the white," he said. "It's heavier. This black stuff is heavy minerals, and it tells us that the sand here came from the Piedmont province. This sand came all the way from Raleigh, or somewhere up there."

Clues were all over the beach. "Look at these shells," said Orrin. "Oysters! Now what's an oyster doing on the beach? The oyster is a soundside animal, found only in estuaries." He picked up an oyster shell and turned it in his hand. "There's only one way he got here naturally. The island rolled over this oyster."

As we walked south through the surf, kicking up fans of water, Orrin said, "We should have the attitude that the changes nature makes in islands aren't bad. When Hurricane Allen passed over Texas, dozens of shallow inlets were cut in Padre Island, and all the newspapers reported this as severe damage. A scientist would have said, 'That's not damage; that's just the way the island evolves.' It's perfectly predictable, and the island is perfectly happy." The tide was coming in, and sunlight shone gold on the dunes. "As long as it's moving and responding to the sea, it's alive," Orrin mused. "A barrier island is really a living thing."

*C*oming home: Former residents of Portsmouth Village arrive in small boats (right) for a rare reunion in the abandoned island town. Margaret McWilliams Smith, who left the village at age 14 and had not returned in nearly seventy years, relives childhood memories with Steve Roberts (below). Founded in 1753 on strategic Ocracoke Inlet, Portsmouth Village once served as North Carolina's principal port of entry. Citizens first abandoned it during the Civil War. Although some returned afterward, the town's population steadily waned. Its last two permanent residents left in 1971. The National Park Service, which now administers Portsmouth as part of Cape Lookout National Seashore, helped arrange this homecoming in the hope that it might become an annual event.

Memories flood back as Margaret McWilliams Smith visits the grave of her brother's close friend. "Everybody had a happy life in Portsmouth," she recalled. "We had everything but money—all the seafood in the world, all the milk and cream we wanted, chickens, eggs, our own hog meat, own beef, and always a nice garden. Our recreation mostly was rowing our boats, riding horses, fishing, playing croquet, and sometimes square dancing."

*B*rimming with life after years of emptiness, Portsmouth's tiny Methodist Church overflows as former residents attend a special reunion service (right). For all, the church formed a major unifying force; for the Willis family (below), it does still. Margaret Willis, a fisherwoman who lived in Portsmouth's abandoned schoolhouse during the mid-1970s, and husband Dallas were married in the church; year-old daughter Caroline was baptized there by the Reverend Jimmy Creech of Ocracoke. A lease now enables them to spend weekends and vacations in Portsmouth. Overjoyed at the homecoming, Margaret said: "It stirs the heart to see the village come back to life, its children coming home, its friends coming to visit, its church full of organ music and singing. The village is like grandparents, always there to come home to."

Weathered driftwood fragment adds stark contrast to the morning sky as the Atlantic

the Southland

By Christine Eckstrom Lee

washes the shore of Cumberland Island, largest of the isles along the Georgia coast.

Islands of South Carolina and Georgia sweep southward in a gentle arc. Usually referred to as sea islands, these flat, often marshy isles contain fertile soil and a wealth of animal life—a combination that attracted settlers from Spain as early as the 16th century. Before the Civil War, southern plantation owners cultivated some sea islands. Around the turn of the century, wealthy Northerners bought many isles for use as hunting retreats. Entrepreneurs have developed a few sea islands, but most retain their untouched character.

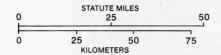

Georgetown

Pawleys Island

SOUTH CAROLINA

South Island

Cape Island

Cape Romain National Wildlife Refuge

Bull Island

Capers Island

Isle of Palms

Charleston

Sullivans Island

Folly Island

Kiawah Island

Port Royal Island

Savannah River

Hilton Head Island

Daufuskie Island

Savannah

Tybee Island

GEORGIA

Wassaw Island

Ossabaw Island

St. Catherines Island

Blackbeard Island

Sapelo Island

Wolf Island

Sea Island

St. Simons Island

Jekyll Island

Little Cumberland Island

Cumberland Island

Cumberland Island National Seashore

FLA.

*T*he loggerhead hatchling raised its head to the sea and blinked. Small enough to hold in a soupspoon, the little turtle was about to swim off into the Atlantic Ocean, an act on the same scale as launching a spaceship into the cosmos—and expecting it to return. I crouched beside the hatchling as a wave swept up and carried it off tumbling and cartwheeling through the surf. At the base of the next breaker, it surfaced for a breath and was gone. Minutes earlier, I had watched a scrambling cluster of hatchling turtles emerge from the sand and run to the sea on the beach of South Island, an oak-and-palmetto-forested island near Georgetown, South Carolina. Protected as part of the state's Tom Yawkey Wildlife Center, South Island is managed primarily as a waterfowl habitat, but its virgin beaches belong to the sea turtles.

If a symbol were to be chosen for the wildness of the islands that shelter the coasts of South Carolina and Georgia—lands known collectively as sea islands—it would be the loggerhead turtle. Of the seven species of sea turtles that roam the world's temperate and tropical waters, six are found in the Atlantic, and all are threatened or endangered. Like all sea turtles, loggerheads nest ashore, and the beaches of the southeastern U. S. make up one of the largest loggerhead rookeries in the world.

On summer nights in the sea islands, when crickets sound a screeching chorus and alligators stir the green waters of inland lagoons, female loggerheads lumber up the beaches like great dark boulders and bury their eggs in the low dunes. About two months later, the hatchlings erupt from beneath the sands and scramble to the waves, guided by the primeval instincts of a creature whose ancestors may date back 150

MAP ART BY SUSANAH B. BROWN

million years. Not long after the Atlantic Ocean was formed, turtles were flippering through the seas. When the Age of Reptiles ended and dinosaurs vanished from the earth, the sea turtle survived.

Under an evening sky of cobblestone clouds, I stood knee-deep in the surf and watched the last tiny loggerhead melt into the waves off South Island. If the hatchling is a female and survives to adulthood, some twenty years from now she will paddle in from the wide reaches of the Atlantic to nest on the beaches along this coast.

The presence of loggerhead hatchlings on South Island is a measure of the nature of the land; the turtles survive here because the island is wild. With its long, empty beaches and its tangled jungle beauty, South Island is like most of the islands that stretch for more than 250 miles along the shores of South Carolina and Georgia. Some three dozen sea islands directly face the Atlantic. Of these, more than half are unspoiled and uninhabited. Some are refuges; others are parks; many have been preserved by private owners.

On a warm October day, when the salt marshes shimmered green-gold in the autumn sun and flocks of ducks darkened the coastal waters, I traveled twenty miles northeast of Charleston, South Carolina, to Cape Romain National Wildlife Refuge. Extending along 25 miles of shore-line, the marshes and islands of Cape Romain encompass more than 34,000 acres, and most of the area is a saltwater wilderness.

To learn about the wildlife and the environments that characterize the sea islands, I had come to tour Bull Island, centerpiece of Cape Romain. I was with the manager of the refuge, George Garris. A 22-year veteran of the U. S. Fish and Wildlife Service, George has worked in Florida, Georgia, and South Carolina, but he feels a special affection for Cape Romain. "I suppose every manager will say this about his own refuge," he told me, "but I think this is the most beautiful stretch of marshland on the whole coast."

Palmetto fronds slapped the windshield as we bounced along the moss-draped trails of Bull Island in a pickup truck and talked about the sea islands. "This island has a list of owners as long as your arm," George said. "In 1936 it was acquired from the Dominick family of New York and made part of the refuge, which had been established in 1932 to provide a resting and feeding place for waterfowl. Until the '30s, there were few such protected areas for wildlife along this coast."

The history of Bull Island is typical of that of most sea islands. Before the Civil War, many of the islands supported plantations. The land yielded indigo, cotton, and rice. During the bankrupt years of Reconstruction, some planters were forced to sell their coastal paradises. Later, wealthy Northerners purchased many islands as hunting reserves. All in all, the land was protected well. But with the 20th century came public pressure for beach access, coupled with concern for the rapid loss of wildlife habitat. Taxes rose, and many island owners sold their lands—some for development, some for preservation. In the islands of Cape Romain, as in numerous other sea islands, wildlife was the victor.

We stopped by the broad marshes at the north end of Bull Island, startling the birds. Dozens of cormorants took to the air, kicking up whitecaps in skipping-stone patterns as they ran across the water and rose into the wind. Three brown pelicans glided past, soaring south on huge wings. "We constantly monitor the pelicans," said George. "Their populations here were so low in the late '60s and early '70s that we

thought we might lose them." As with the peregrine falcons I had seen in Virginia, the pelicans were affected by DDT. The pesticide caused the pelican egg shells to thin, and the species became endangered. "They're coming back," said George. "But even though we have more than 2,800 nests now, the pelican shells are not quite as thick as they were before the mid-'40s. It's taken a long time for the birds to recover."

We watched the pelicans fade into the distance. "Cape Romain is one of the major East Coast nesting sites for the brown pelican," George explained. "Some people call us a little overprotective here. But I'd rather take criticism than lose a species."

Cape Romain's ecological diversity makes it a haven for a variety of threatened and endangered species. Within the boundaries of the refuge every major sea island environment is represented: salt marshes and tidal creeks, freshwater marshes and swamps, lagoons and forests, beaches and dunes—and 30,000 acres of open waters where the more than 250 species of birds that visit the region can fly free.

On a bright blue morning I joined George Garris as he made a routine survey of the refuge by boat. We wound along the creeks of marshy Raccoon Key to Cape Island, a desolate, windswept barrier isle, the seaward outpost of Cape Romain. Monarch butterflies migrating south traced dizzy patterns in the air as we walked along the beach.

"Cape Romain has the densest nesting population of loggerhead turtles on the sea island coast," George said. "A few years ago, we were steadily losing our turtles, and that was really bothering me. Raccoons and high tides were destroying 95 percent of the nests, so last year we decided to move the eggs." George showed me a large wire-mesh pen where he buried the freshly laid loggerhead eggs; about 85 percent of the transplanted eggs hatched.

Spectators crowd near the green at the ninth hole of the Harbour Town Golf Links during the 1981 Sea Pines Heritage Golf Classic, on Hilton Head, South Carolina. Warm, sunny weather and a smorgasbord of recreational activities attract thousands of people yearly to this and other resort islands of the South.

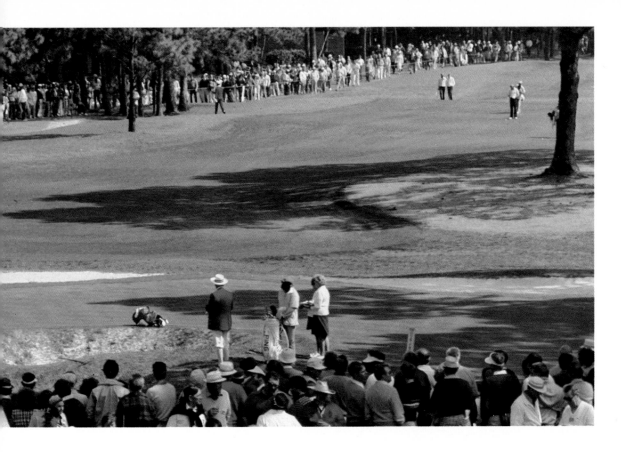

"As natural as these islands are, they haven't been immune to man," George said. "The raccoons are an example. They're eating most of the loggerhead eggs because their population has increased enormously. They have few predators. The bobcats and wolves that helped keep the raccoons in check are gone from most of the islands because of man.

"We have a tremendous responsibility to loggerhead turtles," George said. "And it increases at Cape Romain as nesting areas disappear from the other islands." When sea turtles nest on developed beaches, their hatchlings can become disoriented by the bright lights of homes and the headlights of cars. The hatchlings are then unable to find the sea. "We learn from what happens on other islands," George added, "but we're not taking any chances with our turtles."

The isolation that has helped protect many sea islands and their wildlife has also lured developers over the years. Some islands have been densely developed or dotted with homes for more than a century: Pawleys, Isle of Palms, Sullivans, and Folly in South Carolina, and Tybee, St. Simons, Sea Island, and Jekyll in Georgia have been popular with generations of summer vacationers. From the rustic cottages of Folly Island to the palatial homes of Jekyll's Millionaires Village, the variety in island residences bespeaks the cosmopolitan crowd that journeys to the coast, seeking the magical respite the sea seems to offer.

Yet until the 1950s, other sea islands remained undiscovered, and at least one man feared that when they were, seaside sprawl would mar their shores. His name was Charles Fraser, and his family owned much of Hilton Head Island, in southern South Carolina. In 1957 he began to develop the wilderness of Hilton Head into a planned community, designed to blend in with and preserve the natural environment. The popularity of Fraser's Sea Pines Plantation (Continued on page 146)

*T*iny loggerhead hatchling scuttles across a beach toward the open sea only moments after emerging from its nest among the sand dunes of South Island, South Carolina. Each summer, female loggerheads crawl ashore to lay their eggs in the sand on the wide beaches of the southeastern United States, a primary nesting area for this threatened species and for other sea turtles.

Nutrient-rich salt marsh stretches toward a
maritime forest on South Island. Covered with
luxuriant spartina grass, the marsh nourishes a
profusion of life forms, including plankton,
insects, fish, shellfish, reptiles, and birds.

Full moon ranges above a surreal landscape on Capers Island, South Carolina. An osprey nest

clings to the top branches of a live oak, remnant of a woodland inundated by the advancing sea.

attern for the future: Houses along the ten-mile beach of Kiawah Island, South Carolina (above), rest well back from the ocean. Building the houses behind the secondary dune line leaves the vital dune system intact. Boardwalks such as the one at right provide access to the beach while protecting the vegetation that anchors the sand and stabilizes the dunes against erosion. In 1974 investors from Kuwait bought this 10,000-acre island. Recognizing the sensitive nature of the land, the group commissioned an ecological inventory of the island. The million-dollar study has served as a blueprint for developing Kiawah as a residential community while preserving much of its environment in the natural state.

was astonishing. Over the next two decades Hilton Head's growth mushroomed. Ironically, some residents now worry that the island suffers from too great a demand for homesites and businesses; its resources are strained. Nevertheless, Hilton Head is now a premier vacation destination in the sea islands, and its success has not passed unnoticed by other developers. Many newer resorts have learned from Hilton Head, borrowing and modifying Charles Fraser's principles. Of these resorts, none has received more praise than Kiawah. The wisdom and planning reflected in its development mark Kiawah as a state-of-the-art resort.

Located twenty miles south of Charleston, Kiawah is a 10,000-acre sea island that until 1974 was virtually untouched. In that year the owner, who had purchased Kiawah in 1952 for $125,000, sold the island to the Kuwait Investment Company for 17.4 million dollars in cash—a reflection of the soaring success of both the sea islands and the Middle East petroleum industry. The company wanted to develop the island carefully, and it could afford the time and money to plan the resort. A group of scientists and university professors was hired to prepare an environmental inventory of the island. Over a 12-month period, members of the group analyzed Kiawah, compiling reports on subjects ranging from phytoplankton to loggerhead turtles, from prehistoric Indian sites to geology and coastal processes. They published a 700-page volume of their findings, one of the largest studies ever conducted of a privately owned island, before a single palmetto was cleared for the first villa.

Kiawah's three-phase development was roughly one-third complete when I visited there. I toured the island with Tony Niemeyer, a young Georgian and the Director of Land Development for the Kiawah Island Company. His list of job responsibilities reads like the yellow pages directory for a small town. "I'm in charge of engineering, surveying, and land development," he told me. "And I'm responsible for building roads, water and sewer systems, lakes, marinas, golf courses, and bridges. I also handle archaeology and the loggerhead turtle program."

*W*e drove around the island in Tony's jeep, from the developed phase at the west end to undeveloped areas at the east end, a trip reflecting the planning process from blueprints to reality. "What we're trying to do here on Kiawah is learn to develop and live within the existing natural environment," Tony explained. "It's a tough discipline to understand. I feel very strongly about protecting the environment, and I'm a developer. But you have to understand the land to develop it properly. Planning is the most important thing, and good environmental homework is the key to good planning."

We walked down to the Kiawah River to a dock that serves a new community of cottages. "Look at this river," Tony said. "Isn't it beautiful? Rather than having each one of these homes have their own little dock, we built a community dock. This river could have been spoiled by not thinking far enough ahead. As it is, one dock handles everything."

We drove east along Kiawah's oak-shadowed roads, passing a system of freshwater lagoons that lace the island. "We try to utilize all the opportunities that natural topography offers," Tony said. "These lagoons were built along natural low points in the island—former dune swales. They provide a habitat for alligators, birds, fish; they're pretty; and they're our major storm drainage system."

We continued east along the road. "Look at that tree!" Tony said, stopping the jeep. "This tree tells a story. This is the largest pignut hickory tree in South Carolina. You don't see trees like this very often on barrier islands. See how the road curves around it? This whole road was reengineered and redesigned, the water and sewer systems were rerouted, just so we would miss this tree."

Some of Tony's touches are almost invisible. Kiawah's roads have rounded curbs and curving gutters to drain water, rather than wide ditches along the shoulders. And instead of clearing twenty feet of trees to install sewer lines parallel to the road, Tony designed the pipes to pass under the road. "Ninety percent of the sewer system is under the road," he explained. "Otherwise we would lose trees, shade, and scenery."

We wound along lanes past elegant Kiawah homes; their plans must be approved by an architectural review board. Many houses are nestled deep in the maritime forest, and all beach homes are built behind the secondary dune line. "Everything we do is a multidisciplinary effort," Tony said. "There will never be homes on the beachfront or on the ends of the island because these areas are sensitive. And only 50 percent of Kiawah's land will be developed. We're leaving a lot of open space on the island for wildlife habitat."

One of Kiawah's most protected habitats is the beach. Its wide expanse is a prime nesting site for the loggerhead turtle, and Kiawah has taken unusual steps to ensure that it remains so. Homes near the beach

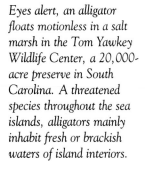

Eyes alert, an alligator floats motionless in a salt marsh in the Tom Yawkey Wildlife Center, a 20,000-acre preserve in South Carolina. A threatened species throughout the sea islands, alligators mainly inhabit fresh or brackish waters of island interiors.

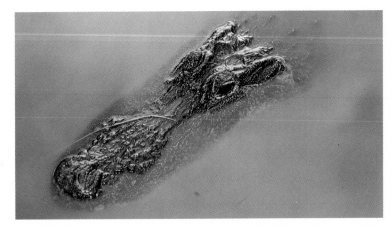

have subdued outside lights so that nesting loggerheads will not be disturbed. Tony has been issued state and federal permits to incubate loggerhead eggs. "I hire two marine biology students to patrol the beaches every night during the May-through-August nesting season," Tony said. The students move the eggs to a wire enclosure like the one I had seen at Cape Romain. "This is our sixth year, and we've been very successful."

Other developers are watching Kiawah's progress. "A group of leading businessmen from all over South Carolina came here to observe what we are doing," Tony said. "And we communicate all the time with other sea island developers to share ideas. Kiawah is exciting to me. I'm watching the evolution of a village by the sea."

The future of another South Carolina sea island remains an anxious question. Daufuskie is a three-by-five-mile island south of Hilton Head and northeast of Savannah, Georgia. Once, before the Civil War, the island was divided into plantations, with gardens and fruit trees and fields of sea island cotton. After the war, the island's economy suffered the fate of the South. Many planters left, and freedmen scraped a hard living from the land. Life on Daufuskie improved in the early part of this century, when island truck farmers sold their produce in Savannah's markets and the oysters from the waters near the island were fancied as the finest in the world. Many of Daufuskie's more than 900 residents harvested oysters or worked in the island's shellfish factory. But after World War II, pollution from the Savannah River ruined the oyster beds; supermarkets undercut the truck farmers; and Daufuskie's population began to decline.

Today many of Daufuskie's 85 residents are retired people or schoolchildren, and most are black. Young men and women usually leave the island to seek jobs. Until recently, few people outside the sea islands even knew that Daufuskie existed. A newspaper story about Daufuskie in 1978 was entitled, "An Island Time Has Forgotten." But in 1980 a group of investors purchased about a third of the island's land for what has been called a "low-density" resort. The residents of Daufuskie suddenly faced the uncertainties that come with being remembered.

To meet some of Daufuskie's residents and learn a little of their lives, I rode over to the island with Bud Bates aboard his shrimp boat, *The Finest Kind*. Bud moved to Daufuskie from Hilton Head in 1975, when he was hired to manage the Daufuskie Island Cooperative Store, the first general store on the island in many years. "Running that store was an education for me," said Bud. "I got to know everyone on the island and hear what things were on their minds." Bud purchased a small wooden house on five acres of land and switched to shrimping two years ago. In the spring of 1981 he married Christina Roth, an artist, and they plan to make Daufuskie their home. "I love this little island," he told me, "and you won't meet finer people anywhere."

We set off on Daufuskie's sandy lanes in Bud's 1956 brakeless jeep to go visiting and were stopped by a herd of cows in the road. "Come on cows. The cows are allowed to roam free all winter," Bud explained. "The only law I know of on this island is that you have to have your livestock in by the time planting season begins. We've got a jail here. It's called the cow jail. If your cow is caught out after the first of March, they put her in a pen and you have to pay $25 to get her out."

Signs along the island's unpaved roads suggest an uncomplicated world: school, church, store, lighthouse, post office, beach. Oxcarts are still used for transportation, and nearly every home has a garden and a grape arbor. Bud honked and stopped to greet everyone along the road. Blossom and Joe Robinson were sitting on their front porch, and Blossom offered us apples, smiles, and a few opinions. "I've got 38 grands, and many great-grands," she said of her family, "and I've got four daughters in Savannah and two here. Every one of my daughters in Savannah would move right back to Daufuskie if there was regular transportation to the mainland." A ferry carries high-school children to the mainland on Monday and brings them home on Friday. There is no other way to get to the mainland except by private boat.

Dressed in dark pants and suspenders, Johnny Hamilton was in his yard with his chickens when Bud and I stopped to visit. A deacon at the island church, Johnny talked of his concern about medical care for the elderly. He was cheered by our visit and (Continued on page 158)

Ox-drawn cart sets an unhurried tempo for Daufuskie Islanders. The isolated island of Daufuskie lies off the southernmost corner of South Carolina, about 15 miles from Savannah, Georgia. In the 1950s pollution from the Savannah River contaminated the rich oyster beds in the waters off Daufuskie, destroying the island's oyster industry. With few jobs available to replace oystering, and no daily ferry service, most islanders left Daufuskie to seek work on the mainland.

Four-room home on Daufuskie Island glows with warmth under the brooding branches

of a centuries-old live oak. The 75-year-old house typifies the simple homes on the island.

*H*is students racing ahead of him, Daufuskie teacher Danny Atkinson (above) nears the Union
Baptist Church during a class outing. Originally a missionary on Daufuskie, Danny now runs a
day-care center for the island's preschoolers, one of whom, 5-year-old Melvin Hazzard (opposite),
strains to chin himself on a swaybacked bar. At left, fourth grader Nicole Smith works on her lessons with
teacher Carol Alberto. Carol and her husband, Jim, teach 17 elementary students in Daufuskie's small
schoolhouse. Carol teaches grades one through four, and Jim teaches five through eight. After finishing the
eighth grade, students must leave the island to continue their education, for Daufuskie has no high school.
On Monday mornings the students travel by boat to the mainland. There they board with families and attend
school during the week, returning home to Daufuskie on Friday evenings.

*C*hannels and creeks meander through broad stands of Spartina alterniflora, or smooth cordgrass, in Bloody Marsh (right). Named for an 18th-century battle between the Spanish and the British, this tidal marsh covers about 1,200 acres on the seaward side of St. Simons Island, Georgia. Marshes such as this one—among the most productive ecosystems in the world—yield as much food energy per acre as a cornfield. In summer, a lavender spiderwort (opposite) spreads delicate petals to the sun along the borders of Bloody Marsh.

Red-jointed fiddler crab, common to spartina marshes, forages in the shallows

of Bloody Marsh. The large claw identifies the $1\frac{1}{2}$-inch-wide crab as a male.

Sparkling white sandbar parallels the shoreline of Little Cumberland Island, Georgia. Privately

owned, Little Cumberland lies at the northern end of the Cumberland Island National Seashore.

said, "It gets so lonely here sometimes. It used to be full of people, so full of people. But it's good to go to the church now and get full of the Lord."

We puttered along the winding roads in Bud's jeep, waving, chatting, and visiting, then stopped at the home of Francis Burn. His family moved to Daufuskie in 1913, when his father was the island lighthouse keeper. "After an absence of 39 years, I came back to stay," he said. Like Bud, Francis is a shrimper, and he discussed the difficulties of working on Daufuskie. "A lot of people couldn't live here for the hardships. It's not easy to survive. Things that go wrong with my boat that would be minor problems on the mainland become disasters here. Life here is that way. If you can't fix it, you just have to learn to Daufuskie-ize."

Francis Burn shares the opinion of a number of islanders in feeling that development would bring a needed boost to the island. "My daddy fought for years for a bridge to this island," he said. "That was his dream. I don't want to see a bridge, but I think we could stand some change, and a few more people to sustain the little store here. Some people want to maintain the status quo. I think others should enjoy the quiet and peace here. This island is Shangri-la."

*I*n the evening I went to see Danny Atkinson, who runs the day-care center for the island's seven preschoolers. A former Californian, Danny first came to Daufuskie in 1975. "I was working with the church then," he explained, "and when I finished school I came back to live here." He told me of his impressions of life on the island. "There may not be jobs on Daufuskie," he said, "but you can't survive here without working. You have to cut wood to keep warm, raise vegetables and livestock, and walk wherever you need to go.

"People help each other so naturally you almost don't notice it. I remember once when Johnny Hamilton went to visit Lillie Simmons. He brought her some okra and she handed him a bag of pecans, and the exchange was simultaneous—they kept right on talking. I cut a tree for Blossom and she sent me a pie. She knows I love pie."

Danny sat inside the children's center, thinking. "Daufuskie may not be rich, but the people are rich. They have respect for one another, they take care of one another, and it's just a beautiful kind of place. A few days ago the developers flew over the island in a helicopter. I heard that they were looking for a golf course site. With those people up there looking down on Daufuskie it's like the hand of God shaping our lives."

The next day, about 25 people attended services at the Union Baptist Church on Daufuskie, and Danny Atkinson served as the minister. A Shaker-style stove warmed the church. About halfway through the service, someone leaned forward and put more wood inside. It was a week before Christmas, and the subject of Danny's sermon was announcements, signs, and prophesies. After the sermon, Johnny Hamilton led a hymn, and the fire inside crackled as the congregation sang, "Come by here, Lord, come by here, O Lord, come by here."

Although the Spanish moss that drapes the shores of Daufuskie is being slowly parted to reveal a glimpse of the land, many of Georgia's sea islands have yet to lift their tangled veils. Bridges connect Tybee, St. Simons, Sea Island, and Jekyll to the mainland, but the rest of Georgia's coastal islands are accessible only by boat. Broad expanses of salt marsh behind the islands have kept them out of sight from the mainland, and until recently private ownership by wealthy families gave many islands a

Red-tiled roofs and lush vegetation lend a Mediterranean flavor to the palatial villas of Sea Island, Georgia. These houses sit dangerously close to the surf. Their owners helped pay for the rock revetment at left, built to protect their lots from erosion and to serve as a buffer against storms. Synonymous with luxurious living, Sea Island has lured the wealthy to its shores since the 1920s.

forbidden-fruit air of mystery. Few people walked the shadowed isles that lay beyond the horizon of marshland prairies.

The names of Georgia's sea islands suggest their complex historical patterns. Some reflect Indian occupation and Spanish settlement: Tybee, Wassaw, Ossabaw; St. Catherines, Sapelo, St. Simons. English colonists named the islands of Jekyll and Cumberland. A hint of the wild days of the buccaneers is preserved by the island called Blackbeard.

A gradual change from private to public ownership has characterized the history of Georgia's islands in recent decades, but the concern of their former owners for their future uses and public awareness of their fragile beauty have combined to keep the islands wild. Wassaw, with its dense virgin forest, and Blackbeard, with its wide beaches and winding foot trails, are open to the public as part of the Savannah National Wildlife Refuge. Ossabaw Island is now a state preserve, and its previous owner maintains a retreat there for artists, writers, and scientists studying island ecology. The E. J. Noble family has set aside St. Catherines for research: Archaeologists are excavating an ancient Indian site on the island, and zoologists there are raising a variety of animals—some of them rare foreign species—for eventual return to the wild.

Sapelo Island was the private domain of the R. J. Reynolds family until the 1950s, when the family established a research foundation on the island. Within a few years, Sapelo's University of Georgia Marine Institute became a pioneering center of research, proving the inestimable value of salt marshes, whose grasses were once considered weeds. Today salt marshes are known to be as productive as an Iowa cornfield. When I toured Sapelo with Marine Institute Director Dr. Don Kinsey, he told me about the importance of Sapelo's research. "Sapelo holds a significant historical niche in science," Dr. Kinsey said, explaining that in large measure the science of ecology originated in the research conducted on the island. "The public's understanding of salt marshes is largely based on the work first done here. As a result, 'salt marsh' has almost become synonymous with the word 'ecosystem'."

To the south of Sapelo, a quiet controversy concerning land use whispers in the forests of Cumberland Island. One hundred years ago, Thomas Carnegie, brother of industrialist Andrew Carnegie, purchased a large portion of the island as a summer retreat, and for a century his family has enjoyed the wild beauty of Cumberland. In 1972 Cumberland was set aside as a national seashore, and most of the island was acquired by the Park Service. Largest of the Georgia sea islands, Cumberland, with 18 miles of pristine beach and 40 square miles of rich forests and marshlands, was prized as the crown jewel of the islands.

Lucy Ferguson, granddaughter of Thomas and Lucy Carnegie, may soon be the only major private landholder on Cumberland. Members of the Candler family of Atlanta, which has long owned a tract of land at the north end of Cumberland, agreed in 1981 to sell their holdings to the Park Service. The management plan for the island calls for the acquisition of all private holdings; the Park Service feels that the future protection of Cumberland is better ensured if the island is managed as a whole. However, Lucy Ferguson does not want to sell her land.

*M*rs. Ferguson greeted me at the door of the Greyfield Inn on Cumberland and spoke softly but plainly as I climbed the steps. "I'm fighting to save my land," she said. "It's the only thing I have in my mind. You would too if you had buried five generations of your family on this island." At 82 years of age, Mrs. Ferguson is lively and spry. Dressed in boots, khaki slacks, and a knit cap, she drove around the island in her open jeep, her poncho whipping in the breeze. Greyfield, a spacious country house built in 1902, was her home until recent years, when she converted it into an inn; she now lives at her farm on Cumberland, a place she calls Serendipity.

"We love Cumberland Island," she told me as we drove along the main road, "and my land means more to me than any amount of money. I think we have the most beautiful beach on the whole Atlantic Coast, and I don't blame the Park Service for wanting Cumberland. But the only reason they have it wild and beautiful is because that's the way we've kept it and loved it." As we drove around the island, Mrs. Ferguson pointed out favorite sights. "Isn't the live oak the most beautiful tree?" she said. "Don't you love the bird tracks in the dunes?" She also spoke of her concern over the management of the land, of the growing numbers of visitors to Cumberland, and about her fear of damage to the island. "I've got to keep working and fighting," she said. "I've got too much to do for an old woman. But it's kept me from mildewing."

We stopped at Plum Orchard, a former family home, and walked around the grounds. The property is now part of the national seashore. We peered through a dusty window into the dining room.

"Once when I was a little girl there was a marvelous party here," Mrs. Ferguson said. "Back in those days they wore beautiful slippers dyed to match their dresses. The guests were here in the dining room, and I crawled into the room and under the table to look at all those

Patrolling the beaches of Cumberland Island, Carol Ruckdeschel searches for stranded animals. A self-trained naturalist, Carol specializes in the study of loggerhead turtles. She records data on stranded loggerheads and reports her findings to the Smithsonian Institution and the National Marine Fisheries Service.

wonderful shoes." She whispered with glee, "Nobody knew I was there!"

We walked back to her jeep and hopped in. Mrs. Ferguson gazed at the house and the trees. "I want to save my land for my children," she said. "It means so much to me. Of my 18 grandchildren, most of them have their hearts here. We are part of the history of the island. We are the last thing left. I think the national parks are necessary, especially for the poor city man. But we are the people who love Cumberland Island. I would like my family to have my land. Does that seem so unfair?"

Her little dog, Ugly, suddenly jumped from the jeep and ran toward some hikers. "Ugly, come back! It's a federal offense!" she cried. "Come here Ugly, pup-pup-pup-pup!" Ugly kept running and she called to one of the hikers to try to catch him. A young woman carried him back to the jeep. "I think you're awfully nice to do this," said Mrs. Ferguson. "Where are you from?"

"Atlanta," said the hiker.

"What do you do there?"

"I'm a counselor," said the young woman.

"I'm so glad to meet you," said Mrs. Ferguson. "Are you keeping warm enough at night here?"

"Oh yes, ma'am."

Mrs. Ferguson turned to me. "Did you know that the campers have to carry in all their water? I'm trying to do something about that. They should dig wells for the campers. And they should have fire rings. They can't dry their clothes at night if they're wet. They should be able to build a fire in a nice big sandy ring and dry off. Don't you think?"

She turned to the young woman. "How do you like Cumberland?"

"It's just beautiful."

"I'm so glad you feel that way. I think so too."

From atop a high dune of flour-soft sand, the landscape was dreamy. The sea was silken and calm, stretching to the horizon in a gentle curve, where it melted into the blue of the sky. Horses grazed in the low dunes, among scattered palmettos and cedars. Nearby, a mountain of sand rolled into the maritime forest—a storm wave frozen at its crest. Gazing at the scene before me I could not help but feel that in the battle of Cumberland, somehow the island has won.

*L*ive oaks, permanently bent and pruned by ocean breezes and salt spray, cling tenaciously to dunes on Cumberland Island (right). Below, rippled waves of sand on a broad Cumberland beach roll toward a horizon dotted with cabbage palms. Famous for its beauty, Georgia's southernmost island looks much the same today as it did a hundred years ago, when Thomas Carnegie purchased large tracts of Cumberland. Over the years the Carnegie family and other landowners preserved much of the forty-square-mile island in its undeveloped state. In 1972 the U. S. Park Service began buying the land after Congress designated Cumberland a national seashore. Today more than 90 percent of the island remains in public trust. The Park Service limits the number of visitors here to ensure that Cumberland Island will retain its wild beauty.

Swooping gulls snatch food tossed by a youngster at Cocoa Beach, south of Cape Canaveral.

a Sweep of Keys

By Christine Eckstrom Lee

Florida's many Atlantic barrier beaches attract sun-seeking visitors from around the world.

A marsh hawk soared above the orange grove, the tips of his wings spread like fingers, his eyes surveying an incongruous domain. Beyond the orange grove stretched thousands of acres of marshes, swamps, and woodlands—primeval places where alligators glide and bobcats stalk; only two miles east of the grove, just inland from the roar of Atlantic waves, a sleek winged vehicle towered above the surrounding lagoons and scrublands. Representing the pinnacle of American space technology, the vehicle stood upended on a concrete pad, ready for its first launch. With sunlight winking on its surface, the space shuttle *Columbia* pointed to the stars.

The land that shelters both the marsh hawk and the space shuttle is Merritt Island, Florida. Located about halfway down the state's eastern coast, Merritt Island forms the broad midsection of a barrier system that curves out from the mainland like a single scallop of lace. At the easternmost point of this formation lies Cape Canaveral, familiar as the place where America launched its space age.

As might be expected in an area where space age and wilderness meet, land use on Merritt Island is as complex as the winding inland waters that ribbon this sandy expanse. A tract covering more than 140,000 acres of the Merritt Island area is shared by the National Aeronautics and Space Administration's John F. Kennedy Space Center, the Merritt Island National Wildlife Refuge, and the Canaveral National Seashore—three groups that would appear to have few ideas in common.

Orange groves add a final twist to the Merritt Island land maze. Roughly 2,500 acres of Merritt Island's wildlife refuge are managed as citrus groves. The groves are leased by the federal government to Florida growers, some of whose families owned groves on Merritt when the notion of sending a man to the moon was only an H. G. Wells fantasy.

In the cool shade of a citrus tree, I watched the marsh hawk wheeling overhead, and I felt that I was in the last and tiniest box inside a series of progressively larger boxes: an orange grove within a wildlife refuge on a barrier formation where U. S. rockets blast off from earth to explore the frontiers of space. Yet to me, Merritt Island represents the curious blend of preservation and growth—of past, present, and future tumbled together—that defines the coastal islands of Florida.

Florida's Atlantic isles and keys extend for more than 500 miles, from Amelia Island at the Georgia border to the Marquesas Keys at the edge of the Gulf of Mexico. Some of the beaches along the eastern Florida peninsula are actually not islands but long thin barrier spits attached to the mainland like streamers. Inland tidal lagoons parallel the coast between the barrier beaches and the mainland. These lagoons are often called rivers: the Matanzas River by St. Augustine; the Halifax River behind the Daytona Beach strand; the Banana River between Cape Canaveral and Merritt Island; the Indian River, running for 125 miles south from Merritt Island's western shore.

The Florida coast is an island parade. The northeast shore has isles like the sea islands of South Carolina and Georgia. From the central coast to Miami the barrier strands resemble the narrow isles of North Carolina's Outer Banks. Southwest of Miami, a luminous chain of coral and limestone keys curls off the tip of Florida like a solar flare. One facet of the variety in Florida's islands is their vegetation: Both temperate zone plants and lush subtropical growth are found along the coast. On Merritt Island, the two vegetation zones overlap.

Rich in contrast, Florida's Atlantic isles hug 350 miles of coast, then curve to the west in a 170-mile-long archipelago edging the Gulf of Mexico. The antebellum plantations on Amelia and Fort George Islands to the north yield to windswept dunes and marshes on Merritt Island, home of the John F. Kennedy Space Center. In the south, Miami Beach opens the way to the Florida Keys, a chain of limestone and coral islands sheltering the endangered Key deer, the great white heron, and other animals. Sultry Key West, the southernmost point in the continental United States, offers beaches, boutiques, and a lively nightlife.

MAP ART BY SUSANAH B. BROWN

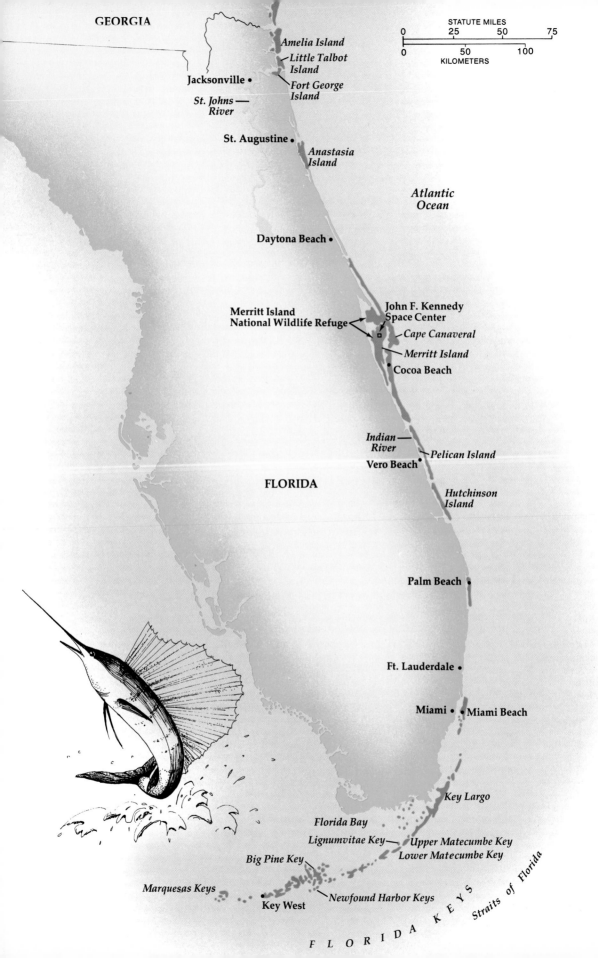

GEORGIA

Amelia Island

Little Talbot
Island

Jacksonville •

Fort George
Island

St. Johns —
River

St. Augustine •

Anastasia
Island

Atlantic
Ocean

Daytona Beach •

STATUTE MILES
0   25   50   75

0   50   100
KILOMETERS

John F. Kennedy
Space Center

Merritt Island
National Wildlife Refuge

Cape Canaveral

Merritt Island
Cocoa Beach

Indian
River

Pelican Island

Vero Beach •

FLORIDA

Hutchinson
Island

Palm Beach •

Ft. Lauderdale •

Miami • • Miami Beach

Key Largo

Florida Bay

Lignumvitae Key —

Upper Matecumbe Key

Lower Matecumbe Key

Big Pine Key

Marquesas Keys

Newfound Harbor Keys

Key West

F L O R I D A   K E Y S

Straits of Florida

Merritt Island's vistas are at once familiar and foreign. Walking through the pine woodlands on a whistling February day, I could imagine I was in a Maine forest; a pine-needle carpet muffled my footsteps. Along the Black Point Wildlife Drive, I looked out over fields of salt marsh to dense hammocks of cabbage palms, cedars, and hardwoods scattered across the grasslands. Around a loop in the trail, mangrove islands humming with insects crouched bent-kneed in dark shallows. The waters fluttered white with the wings of herons and egrets—a scene from a faraway tropical land. In the distance, above a fringe of palmettos shivering in the wind, rose the massive cube of NASA's Vehicle Assembly Building, where engineers put together the space shuttle.

"In the shadow of all this advanced space technology is this unique natural area that shelters a dozen threatened or endangered species of animals," said Dorn Whitmore, an outdoor recreation planner for the Merritt Island National Wildlife Refuge. "Merritt Island has a tremendous variety of wildlife. One reason is the huge array of coastal habitats we have here," Dorn explained. "We have everything from oak hammocks to mangrove islands—and a whole Noah's Ark of animals, including some 280 species of birds."

As Dorn and I set off to explore the refuge and space center lands, our first path led to an orange grove. Pointing up to a tree spangled with bright fruit, Dorn said, "The oranges grown in this part of Florida are considered by some to be the best in the world." Later I sampled an orange grown on Merritt. Slicing off its top, I squeezed the center like a sponge and drank the juice. The flavor was sweet and delicate.

Merritt Island's citrus groves are a living part of Florida history. Ponce de León first touched the coast of Florida in 1513— in search of gold and the Fountain of Youth; when he returned in 1521, he may have scattered the first orange seeds here. Spanish explorers and sailors carried citrus seeds with them on their voyages, introducing oranges and other fruit to the New World. In Florida's warm climate, wild orange trees flourished.

"In the early 1830s, a man named Douglas Dummett was traveling up the Indian River, between Merritt Island and the mainland," Dorn explained. "And the story goes that he smelled wild orange blossoms perfuming the air and decided to stay. Here on Merritt Island, Dummett pioneered the Indian River citrus industry." Connoisseurs of Florida citrus speak of Indian River fruit with an almost mystical reverence. Its fanciers call it "finer," "juicier," "the crème de la crème."

The success of Dummett's citrus grove attracted other growers to Merritt Island, while the island's abundant wildlife lured hunters and fishermen who established private clubs here during the first half of this century. That same era marked the beginning of the Florida land boom. Coastal development swept inexorably northward from Miami, toward the orange groves and sportsmen's preserves of Merritt Island. Then in the 1950s a team of scientists and engineers began launching missiles from a modest base on Cape Canaveral. At about the same time that real estate speculators started to eye the unspoiled lands of Merritt Island for development, the U. S. space program gained momentum, and NASA turned its gaze from the confines of Cape Canaveral to the open spaces of Merritt Island. They needed room to send a man to the moon.

"It may seem ironic, but NASA is the only reason this wildlife refuge

Twilight shadows deepen over Kingsley Plantation, on Fort George Island, near Jacksonville. The frame manor house dates from the early 19th century, when slave trader Zephaniah Kingsley lived here. Despite his occupation, Kingsley wrote staunch defenses of the rights of freedmen, and he himself took the daughter of an East African tribal chief as his wife. Flags of four nations—France, Spain, Britain, and the United States—have flown over Fort George Island since the French landed here in 1562.

exists," Dorn Whitmore said as we drove toward the sprawling Kennedy Space Center complex. "In 1962 NASA acquired 140,000 acres of Merritt Island to expand their operations and to serve as a buffer zone for the launches," he explained. "Then in 1963, NASA began turning over lands not used for its buildings and operations to the U. S. Fish and Wildlife Service for a refuge. NASA still owns the land, but we now manage all but 10,000 acres used by the Kennedy Space Center for their base facilities. That makes Merritt Island the largest refuge on the Atlantic Coast."

The coexistence of wildlife biologists and aerospace engineers on Merritt requires that Dorn know about solid-rocket boosters as well as coastal hardwood hammocks. Our conversation—and our path—zigzagged from the refuge to the space center. We stopped near the space shuttle launch pad. Of the 12 threatened or endangered species of animals that inhabit Merritt Island, 10 can be sighted within a few hundred yards of the spot where the shuttle was soon to lift off into space: Three species of sea turtles nest on the beach near the site; indigo snakes slither in the scrub behind the dunes; manatees, alligators, and salt marsh snakes swim in the nearby lagoons; brown pelicans, peregrine falcons, and bald eagles fly high around the space shuttle monolith.

"Of course we are concerned about the environmental impact of the launches," said Dorn, "but so is NASA. We'll both be monitoring the wildlife, and especially the effect of the acid dust cloud that forms when the shuttle is launched—although we probably won't know the full impact for some time."

Just before dawn on April 12, 1981—at T minus two hours and counting—the roads in and around Merritt Island were packed bumper-to-bumper, sneaker-to-sneaker. More than half a million people stared to the eastern horizon. Against a clear black *(Continued on page 178)*

H̵igh-stepping Louisiana heron (right) strides through rich wetlands in the Merritt Island National Wildlife Refuge. In another part of the refuge, a white mangrove (top) struggles to survive in a dried-up marsh—graphic evidence of the drought plaguing the area in 1981. The drought dramatically affected the usually wet and lush refuge. Microscopic plants and animals, essential parts of the food chain, perished as the wetlands shrank. The dry conditions forced some birds to abandon the refuge and disturbed the nesting habits of others. Wintering on Merritt Island, a greater yellowlegs (above) scurries across the parched soil.

*S*pace shuttle Columbia (right) thunders away from the Kennedy Space Center, on Merritt Island. Floodlights bathe the shuttle, and lights twinkle on its support structure (below, left) as workers toil through the night before the final countdown on April 12, 1981. A newspaper photographer (below, right) checks his cameras before the launch. More than half a million observers watched the history-making lift-off in person; millions of others saw it on TV. After a 54-hour flight and 36 orbits of the earth, the first reusable space vehicle made a smooth landing in California, ushering in what astronaut John W. Young, commander of the mission, terms "routine access to space."

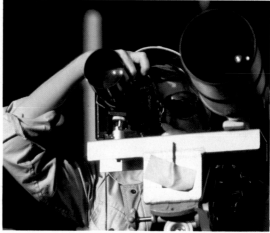

JON SCHNEEBERGER, TED JOHNSON, JR., AND ANTHONY PERITORE, NATIONAL GEOGRAPHIC STAFF (RIGHT)

Snowy egret, its reflection shimmering in evening light, stalks its marsh-dwelling prey in the

Merritt Island refuge, home also to endangered brown pelicans, peregrine falcons, and bald eagles.   175

*P*alm-fringed pool at the Fontainebleau
Hilton and azure waters of the nearby
Atlantic create a swimmer's paradise for Miami
Beach vacationers (right). On the beach in front
of the 1,200-room hotel, Nancy Beckwith sells
and applies suntan lotion to a winter-pale guest
(above). Each winter the population of Miami
Beach increases tenfold, fulfilling the vision of
entrepreneur Carl Fisher, who changed what was
once a mangrove-covered wilderness into one of the
most popular vacation spots in the United States.

sky, the world's most intense spotlights illuminated the glowing white space shuttle. No one turned his gaze away from it for long; it tempted the eyes like a solar eclipse. As dawn spread across the sky, the loudspeaker announcer counted, "Five, four, three. . . ."

After that, I remember hearing nothing but screams. Huge clouds of black-and-white smoke mushroomed around the launch pad as the space shuttle *Columbia* zoomed into the sky atop an incandescent pyramid of flame. The ground rumbled, I shuddered, and the air popped and cracked as a roaring wall of sound enveloped me. People yelled, hooted, whistled, clapped, cheered, and cried with joy as the space shuttle arced across the dome of the sky and slowly faded into the blue beyond.

For a nation that has grown with the sense of an expanding frontier, the space shuttle points the way to the widest horizons of all. Watching the shuttle soar into the sky, I found it hard to imagine that, less than two centuries ago, the Florida coast itself was an American frontier. In the islands of northeastern Florida, tales of the past are often told in present tense. History here is pervasive—and tangible—from Indian shell-heaps to colonial plantations. When the U. S. acquired Florida from Spain in 1821, the islands of Amelia, Little Talbot, and Fort George had been a crossroads of colonizers for more than 250 years. Located just south of the Georgia border—once the boundary between the American colonies and Spanish Florida—the northeast isles hold traces of Indian, French, Spanish, British, and American occupation. Their history is a rollicking pageant of the events that shaped Florida.

"**F**lorida was once a formidable place," said historian Dena Snodgrass. "With its great forests and swamps, it was a difficult land for the early Europeans to settle. Everyone wanted Florida, but no one wanted to live here! It was even said that no one would immigrate to Florida—not even from hell itself. Isn't that unbelievable now!" We sat in Dena's Jacksonville apartment and talked about "old Florida." Dena is the past president of both the Jacksonville and the Florida Historical Societies. A former schoolteacher and research economist, she is now active in historical work. When she taught school she would tell the children, "Florida became a part of the U. S. in 1821. That was the year my grandmother was born. I knew her and could touch her. Now you know me, and when you touch my hand—bing! We just spanned the whole U. S. history of Florida!"

Fort George Island, near the mouth of the St. Johns River, has a special fascination for Dena. "The story of Fort George is a capsule of the history of Florida," she told me. Timucuan Indians were living on Fort George when the French landed on the island in 1562. The French built a fort nearby in 1564—a year before the Spanish founded St. Augustine, America's oldest surviving European settlement. Later, Fort George was the site of a Spanish mission, a British fort, and a colonial plantation.

Fort George is quiet now, sleepy in the Florida sun, tangled with moss and palmettos, and thick with the eerie stillness of a stadium after the crowds have left. I walked into early 19th-century Florida when I visited the Kingsley plantation on the northern shore of the island. Now a state historic site, the Kingsley manor home is the oldest existing plantation house in Florida—and the former residence of a colorful figure.

"Zephaniah Kingsley was quite a character," said Superintendent Winton Keeth, as we walked through the restored rooms of the Kingsley

Hotels and condominiums front a narrow strip of sand on Miami Beach. Early developers here flattened protective dunes. By the beginning of the 1970s the beach had nearly vanished through erosion. Though state and federal officials concede the difficulty of fighting such erosion, they continue efforts to protect this major urban center. In 1977 the U. S. Army Corps of Engineers joined Florida in a 67-million-dollar project to restore and maintain the fragile beach that separates the high rises from the sea.

home. "He was a slave trader, but he married Anna Jai, an East African princess. Kingsley believed that slavery was an economic necessity, yet he wrote that its abuses were revolting."

Kingsley owned several boats that traveled up and down the St. Johns River providing transportation and carrying goods to trade or sell to plantation owners. Florida was Spanish when he bought Fort George in 1817; he claimed loyalty to Spain. But after the U. S. acquired Florida, he was appointed to the territorial legislature by President James Monroe—as a loyal American. The truth about Kingsley is still debated.

Years later, in 1886, a luxury hotel opened on Fort George Island. It was a harbinger of the land-and-resort boom that fashioned the fate of modern Florida. In the 1890s financier Henry Flagler completed a railroad from Jacksonville to Miami, built resort hotels in St. Augustine, Palm Beach, and Miami, and triggered the landslide of development that forever changed the Florida coast.

Ironically, it was from Florida—the newest East Coast state—that a cry first arose for the U. S. government to preserve a piece of Atlantic coastal land. At the turn of the century, plume hunters and commercial fishermen were destroying brown pelicans and their nests on a tiny Indian River isle midway between Cape Canaveral and Palm Beach. In 1903 Theodore Roosevelt established three-acre Pelican Island as our nation's first national wildlife refuge.

"Pelican Island made people realize that we need some places where we can look after the land and the wildlife," said Lawrence Wineland as we motored up the Indian River. Lawrence was the manager of Pelican Island from 1964 until his retirement in 1980. "We have to take some responsibility for what we do, especially here in Florida," he said. "This is one of the most fragile states we have, and it's changing so fast I hardly know where I am when I wake up in the morning." He lowered his voice to a hush. "Here come the pelicans!"

Hundreds of pelican heads poked up like periscopes from low mangrove shrubs as we glided ashore on the island. Mothers swooped and shrieked, and the island burst to life, a screaming jungle of pelicans.

Downy chicks perched in the bushes, flapping flightless wings, straining their necks to squawk the sort of long, loud, rising cry that a horror movie director might want to hear from his terrified heroine.

Lawrence smiled at the birds, unfazed by the commotion. "In this warm climate, we have baby birds born ten months a year," he said. "There are about 300 nesting pairs here now, but they're decreasing, like the mangroves. When I first came here the mangroves were so tall I could walk underneath them, and now they're dying out. But it's just a cycle. Pretty soon they'll come back, and so will lots more pelicans. I don't worry about anything that's a natural phenomenon. The pelicans were here long before I was, and they'll be here long after I'm gone."

Later we drove south toward Vero Beach, along the barrier island that shelters Pelican. The barrier island has no name; its label is the collective sum of the beach towns and developments that line its shores. We passed lands staked for development, houses in various stages of construction, then reached dense condominium projects. "A lot of this land used to be citrus groves," said Lawrence. "Land over here is so expensive it should sell by the inch. When you sell it for real estate development, that's the end of the story. What will be left for the children?"

Buildings grew taller as we drove farther south. "There wasn't a high rise here when I came," said Lawrence. When I asked how far south the development extended, Lawrence said simply, "To Miami." We turned around and drove north along the inland shore of the Indian River. Skeins of pelicans sailed toward Pelican Island. "Look at those birds. Beautiful!" said Lawrence. "Their wingspans are so great they can just

Overseas Highway spans cobalt blue waters between Upper Matecumbe Key, foreground, and Lower Matecumbe Key, at top. Built in the 1930s along a railroad bed destroyed by a hurricane, the 159-mile highway links Key West to the mainland. Developments such as the complex at lower left have changed the face of many islands. Lignumvitae Key, at upper right, preserves terrain undisturbed since 16th-century Spanish explorers first glimpsed these islands.

Captain Bob West of the charter boat Sea Dancer *holds a thrashing barracuda at arm's length as he carefully removes his hook. Fishing only for sport in shallow spawning grounds a few miles from Key West, the veteran guide returned the ten-pound barracuda to the sea. Waters of the lower keys challenge anglers with some of the world's most exciting sportfishing.*

glide forever. Pelicans are such nice old birds. They don't seem to mind all the new people here. They're pretty tough, but changes in their environment can really hurt them. That's why they're vulnerable. You could say that Florida and the pelican have something in common."

I saw the development that Lawrence decries as I drove south to Miami along the coast. My route paralleled the railroad Flagler built to open southern Florida to settlement. In 1900 Florida's population was half a million; since 1970 alone, the state's population has grown by nearly six times that number. As a result of Florida's rapid growth, the state's land and water resources are stretched taut. Everyone seems to want to relax on a patch of sand toasted by Florida sunshine. Near the end of Flagler's coastal line, in Miami, rises the jagged skyline of Miami Beach, mecca for refugees from northern winters and the most densely developed barrier island on the Atlantic Coast.

Southwest of Miami lies Florida's island fantasy world: the keys. From Key Largo to Key West, the islands curve for more than a hundred miles between the Straits of Florida and the Florida Bay, forming a beckoning finger of isles that graze the Gulf of Mexico. The keys rest low in iridescent aquamarine shallows, their greenery drab beside the embarrassing beauty of the surrounding waters.

The Overseas Highway spans the length of the keys, ending in Key West. One of its bridges crosses seven miles of water. Traveling the road gave me the odd sense of driving out to sea. This route is the last legacy of Henry Flagler, who completed a railroad to Key West in 1912 in the face of claims that it couldn't be done. A hurricane destroyed the railroad in 1935, and a highway was built along its former bed. Development slowly traced lines on each side of the route, and the isolated, 19th-century dreamworld of the keys was unveiled.

One island midway in the keys was not linked to the overseas line. Miraculously, modern development passed by the 280-acre key called Lignumvitae. Now preserved as a state botanical site, Lignumvitae Key is one of the last remaining examples of how (Continued on page 188)

*G*narled roots of the lignum vitae, or "wood of life," cling
to the limestone surface of Lignumvitae Key (above).
Accessible only by boat and now a protected state
botanical site, the island abounds in life. Roots of another
hardwood, the gumbo-limbo (left), spread over a wide area to
give support to the tree and to find sustenance in the sparse
topsoil. The four-inch-wide golden orb weaver (opposite) spins
a web up to five feet across. The spider's silk, one of the
strongest known natural fibers, can ensnare lizards and birds.
Bright bands gleaming, a Florida tree snail (right) inches along
a lignum vitae branch in search of lichens and algae to eat.

*B*lue skies and glistening waters for a backdrop, beachgoers play volleyball on the coral sands of Key West's Smathers Beach (below). Island resident Lisa Halloran joins Keith Sciandra for a splashing stroll along the water's edge (opposite, bottom). At the Sands Beach Club, visitors set a more sedate pace, relaxing on lounge chairs (left). "The Last Resort," some call Key West. Once the domain of pirates, rumrunners, and "wreckers"—islanders who salvaged the cargoes of ships that foundered on the treacherous reefs nearby—Key West now attracts refugees from frigid northern winters.

"*I* do what people like about Key West, and people like the old Key West," Mario Sanchez remarks, wielding a chisel and a mallet with skilled hands. Slowly "Blues in a Basket" emerges from a slab of red cedar (below). Since the 1930s Sanchez has carved images from the island's past and present, painting them in brilliant colors. A native Key Wester, the artist descends from Cubans who came here in the 1860s to open cigar factories. In the scene above, a lector atop a platform reads to workers as they roll cigars. The lector broke the tedium of the factory and educated the workers at the same time. Now known for his artistry after years of obscurity, Sanchez receives several thousand dollars for each of his creations. His newfound recognition pleases him, yet he says, "I don't want to be famous. I'm just Mario."

wild all the Florida Keys were when the Calusa Indians first looked across the Straits of Florida and saw Spanish ships on the horizon.

"This island is the prize of the Florida Keys," said Ranger Jeanne Parks, a young wildlife ecologist. We hiked into the heart of the island. "We're walking through a tunnel of time," she said. Gnarled arms of gumbo-limbo and poisonwood trees entwined in the woods, their trunks covered with peeling multicolored bark. Jeanne showed me striped tree snails, splashy butterflies, huge spiders, and the island's namesake tree.

"The keys are the northern limit of the lignum vitae tree," said Jeanne. "This forest has the layered canopies and the diversity of the tropics, but things don't grow as big. The trees here are like bonsai plants. *Lignum vitae* is Latin for 'wood of life.' The Spanish thought the tree's wood was magic because it sinks in water. Lignum vitae is no longer harvested in the U. S. because it's too hard to find." Muscular branches curved from one trunk a little more than a foot in diameter. "This tree is probably 1,400 years old," said Jeanne. "Think how the keys have changed around this tree. It's amazing that this island is still wild. You won't see anything else like it. This is the real Florida Keys."

Lignumvitae's counterpoint is Key West, a delightfully eccentric island town. Every day there was a surprise, but after a while, I expected to see the unexpected: clowns on unicycles pedaling down the road, fishermen dancing on restaurant tables, mimes and jugglers performing in the streets, a thirsty customer walking into a bar on his hands. One resident told me, "Key West is like living in a carnival."

Each evening a zany cast of characters teams up with Mother Nature to provide one of Key West's wildest shows, a ritual known as "Sunset." At dusk crowds gather at Mallory Square, a pier at the island's west end, to watch the sun dip into the sea and to enjoy the exuberant shows of the street-theater performers who appear there. Jugglers, gymnasts, comics, mimes, musicians, and dancers all display their talents on Mallory Square's outdoor stage, against a backdrop of exploding twilight colors that transform Key West into a wonderland.

As I stood in Mallory Square, vendors were selling orange juice and jewelry while the sun lowered to the horizon. An elderly black man on an old yellow bicycle rode by, calling out his wares: "Hot banana bread! Conch salad! Peanuts!" The "Iguana Man" strolled among the crowds, stroking two pet iguanas draping his shoulders. Everybody was laughing and smiling.

Will Soto, a juggler, tossed a torch to the ground to begin his show. People formed a circle around him, stomping, clapping, and yelling as he performed juggling feats and magic tricks, finishing his act by juggling a torch, a machete, and an apple—and eating the apple between tosses. "I dedicate this to street theater!" Will said. "And to Key West for supporting street theater!" He blew a whistle. "To Key West!" A double cheer arose as Will ended his show—and the sun set.

Creative energy charges Key West. The town's freewheeling pace has always attracted artists, writers, and musicians. One of the island's most famous residents was Ernest Hemingway. He wrote some of his best-loved books at his spacious home in Key West. Hemingway immortalized his favorite watering hole, Sloppy Joe's, in *To Have and Have Not*. Though the bar is now called Captain Tony's Saloon, Hemingway would undoubtedly recognize the place he once knew.

"This is a town where you can be anybody you want," said Captain Tony. "You could have three heads and nobody would bother you. That's why I love Key West." Dressed in khaki pants and a T-shirt, Tony sat at his bar and watched the people walking in the door, many stopping to greet him. "When people are away from home in a place like Key West, their true selves come out. I see it happen every day."

Tony's humor—and his life—are displayed on the cluttered walls of his saloon: Buoys and sea memorabilia symbolize his early days as a shrimper in Key West; the signboard from his old charter fishing boat, the *Greyhound IV,* hangs near the pool tables; newspaper articles and pictures from a movie based on his life patch the walls, along with posters from his two unsuccessful mayoral campaigns. "I ran barefoot, I had a beard, and I kissed the mothers instead of the babies," he said.

When Tony came to the island in 1948, "Key West was like the Barbary Coast—a wild, rip-roaring town," he said. "It didn't seem like it belonged to the United States." In time, Tony came to love the natives of the keys, the Conchs.

"I realized that Key West wasn't the coconut trees or the beaches or the flowers—it was the people. This is a hard place to survive in, and the struggle has made the people beautiful. Now everything is changing so fast—they're putting up new buildings all over. But the Conchs know what will happen. There's an old Conch saying, 'The wheel has to turn,' and when the wheel comes around a hurricane will knock Key West right back to being a fishing village. The Conchs have been here for hundreds of years and they know. The past is very important here."

Key West's nickname, "The Last Resort," suggests the history of leaps and drops in its fortunes that have forced islanders to improvise. At the Key West Library, I talked with Betty Bruce, a local historian and a Conch. Easygoing and charming, she told me about Key West's early days, punctuating the telling with her deep, rich laugh.

"Key West has been a boom-and-bust town," said Betty. "Once we were the richest town in Florida. During the Depression we were the poorest. In 1890 we were the largest city in Florida, during the heyday of the cigar industry. When war broke out in Cuba in 1868, the cigar makers moved from Havana to Key West. Later the cigar makers moved to Tampa, but we still have a good-size Cuban community here."

One day I visited Mario Sanchez, a Cuban primitive artist. He stood in the shade of a sapodilla tree, mallet and chisel in hand, carving a basket of fish from a slab of red cedar resting on his easel—an old sewing machine table. I had seen prints of his woodcarvings, which show scenes of life in the Key West of his boyhood, re-created entirely from memory. Mario is humble about his fame, and he attributes his success to luck. "What I do is just primitive," he said, tapping at his carving. "Nobody showed me. I got lucky. Half of everything in life is luck, no matter what talent you have. People started liking the things I do, and that's luck." He smiled. "If you like what I do, then I'm lucky again."

Mario's grandfather was a cigar maker who came to Key West in 1868. His father was a reader in a cigar factory: While the workers rolled cigars, Mario's father stood before them and read novels and world newspapers. He showed me a partially completed carving of his father reading. "It was an education for the workers," Mario explained. "The workers paid to hire the reader, and they voted on which novels would be read. When my father finished a book, he'd just have an election.

"My uncle was a cigar maker," said Mario, "And he used to sit and tell me about France, England, Germany—places all over the world that he'd learned about from the reader in the cigar factory. It was just as if he had made a trip there, and he had never been out of Key West."

Mario brushed chips from his carving, and a fish emerged. "You know when you get lucky in this business, you're old," Mario said. "Well I'm looking at this while I'm living. People say, 'You're going to be great when you die.' I say, 'No. I want the flowers while I'm living.'" He looked up and smiled. "I want to smell them now."

For years, one political regime after another in Havana has sent waves of refugees to Key West and to southern Florida. The boat lift from Cuba's Mariel Harbor in the spring of 1980 was only the most recent flight of Cubans to U. S. shores. Early one morning in April 1980, I stood at a dock in Key West and watched a family step off a boat to freedom.

Ten months after the boat lift, I went to Miami to visit them. Celia and Antonino Plasencia, brother and sister, their mother, and Celia's little boy, Rafael, were the last of their family left in Cuba. They had been trying to leave for several years, and when the 1980 exodus began, they seized the opportunity to go. "I think that I am living again," Antonino told me as I arrived at their home. He now has a job as a bookkeeper at a bank, and Celia works as a secretary for the Cuban Agency, helping refugees apply for residence papers in the U. S. "We are so happy to have our whole family together," said Celia. "This is the only country in the world that gives a helping hand to people."

They talked about their voyage to Key West. They left Cuba late at night, hit rough seas, and their boat leaked badly. They feared the boat would sink. "I could only think, 'Oh God, let me see the light again,'" said Antonino. "I was sure we would die. When I saw the blue sky and Key West in the distance, I said, 'Thanks to God.'"

"We left Cuba in order to have liberty," said Celia. "On the bus from Key West to Miami, everything looked beautiful to me. Cuba is not my country anymore. The only thing left for me there is memory."

"When I arrived in the United States, I felt a big relaxation," said Antonino. "Now I am free. I am beginning a new life. This is my second birth." When I left, Celia said to me, "You are always welcome here. Remember, this is your home."

Palm fronds frame the courtyard of Ernest Hemingway's Key West home, now a museum. Attracted like many other artists and writers by the island's genial climate and isolation, the noted author moved here in 1928. By 1935 his house had become a tourist attraction. He wryly called it "all very flattering . . . to the easily bloated ego . . . but very hard on production." The Spanish-colonial-style structure dates from 1851. Museum guides say the cats prowling around the courtyard descend from some of the dozens that Hemingway kept.

Near the end of my island travels, photographer David Harvey and I made a canoe journey with naturalist Stan Becker around the Newfound Harbor Keys. Bordering the Straits of Florida south of Big Pine Key, these islands are a wilderness of mangroves and dunes. The sun shone pink through the wings of a roseate spoonbill gliding over the trees as we paddled across crystalline shallows and through a mangrove tunnel along one island's shore.

Toward dusk, we paddled into the Straits of Florida, an amphitheater of blue sky and sea. The waters were banded in electric blues and greens; a thin silver line traced the horizon. To the west lay Mexico; to the south Cuba; to the east the Bahamas, where Columbus made his first landfall in the New World. Rocking in our canoes, we watched the sun set into a shimmering pink sea as the full moon rose in the east, casting a white spotlight across the darkening waters.

Before us, the Newfound Harbor Keys presented their wild face as we moved toward them in darkness. We felt like explorers. Far off in another time, the voyagers who sailed the wide Atlantic to the New World must have crept up to tangled shores with the same startled thrill we felt paddling in white moonlight toward the islands. In a channel between two keys, a pair of dolphins burst from the waters by our canoes, diving in circles around us, chasing us as we paddled home.

Some say the Atlantic isles are no longer wild, that development has changed them all forever. As flocks of birds blackened the white orb of the moon, I looked around at these rustling keys and knew that some islands will always remain as wild as the seas that shape their shores.

"*I feel these people here . . . still alive . . . many a night when I close at 3:30 or 4 a.m.," muses Tony Tarracino (below) about long-departed patrons of his Key West bar, Captain Tony's Saloon. In the 1930s local characters and such literary notables as John Dos Passos, Max Perkins, and Ernest Hemingway frequented the old saloon, then called Sloppy Joe's. Leaving New Jersey in 1948, Tarracino eventually hitchhiked to Key West on a milk truck from Miami. He never left, becoming owner of the bar in 1963. Tarracino adds pictures of his favorite stars to walls thick with graffiti. "I can never sell this place, no matter how much anyone offers," he says. "It would be like selling my soul." Up the street from Captain Tony's stands the present-day Sloppy Joe's (left), gleaming in neon and featuring Hemingway memorabilia. The author patronized it for a short time before he left Key West in 1940.*

Sunset and sidewalk stars lure a crowd to Key West's Mallory Square at evening. As jugglers

on unicycles toss torches, islanders give a traditional cheer in bidding farewell to the day.

Acknowledgments

The Special Publications Division is grateful to the individuals, organizations, and agencies named or quoted in the text and to those cited here for their generous assistance: Denny Alexander, Eric Allaby, J. Clinton Andrews, Walter S. Barrett, Dennis W. Berg, Albert G. Brock, Lisa Brunetti, John Buckalew, Lisa Cole, John Crawford, Larry Cronin, Chester DePratter, Bernice M. Dickson, Kim Downs, Anne Driessnack, Carl Driessnack, Bob Dunn, Pam Frank, Douglas R. Grant, Bill Harris, Ed Harrison, Gary W. Harvey, Buddy Hasell, Jackie Hasell, Larry Herndon, Marcia Herndon, Mark Hess, Waring Hills, Sally R. Hopkins, Elizabeth Howard, James D. Howard, Robert L. Joyner, Don Kincaid, Donald J. Kosin, Ed Lane, Peter F. Larsen, Fern Leslie, Jim Leslie, Judy Leslie, Raymond Lopez, W. B. McCaskill, Edith H. McCauley, Clay McDaniel, Michael D. McKenzie, John Miller, Edward du Moulin, Steven J. Muzal, Andy Newman, Thomas E. Norton, J. Gordon Ogden III, Robert N. Oldale, Frederick P. Pariani, Jr., Joseph F. Patterson, Warren Pierce, Kathryn Proby, Preston D. Riddel, George C. Rogers, Jr., Cathy Sakas, Susan Saylor, Robert L. Scheina, Steven G. Scott, Al Seeschaft, Foy Shaw, Kevin Shore, Susan Shore, W. E. Smith, Dian Joy Spitler, Edouard A. Stackpole, James St. Pierre, Lydia Swift, Woodrow Thompson, Wesley N. Tiffney, Bruce Weber, Laura Weigle, Larry Williams, S. Jeffress Williams, Pat Young; Little Talbot Island State Park, Loco-Motion Vaudeville, Long Key State Recreation Area, National Park Service, Smithsonian Institution.

Gulls wheel above an angler surf-casting on a Nags Head beach in North Carolina's Outer Banks. Stretching some 180 miles along the coast, this slender barrier chain helps shield the mainland from storms.

Index

Boldface indicates illustrations.

Library of Congress CIP Data

Morrison, H. Robert.
  America's Atlantic isles.
  Bibliography: p.
  Includes index.
  1. Atlantic coast (United States)—Description and travel. 2. Islands—Atlantic coast (United States) 3. Maritime Province—Description and travel. 4. Islands—Maritime Province. 5. Morrison, H. Robert. I. Lee, Christine Eckstrom. II. National Geographic Society (U. S.). Special Publications Division. III. Title.
F106.M85   975'.00942   80-7828
ISBN 0-87044-364-X (regular binding)   AACR2
ISBN 0-87044-369-0 (library binding)

Additional Reading

The reader may wish to consult the National Geographic Society Index for articles, and to refer to the following books: Pat Conroy, *The Water is Wide;* E. Norman Flayderman, *Scrimshaw and Scrimshanders: Whales and Whalemen;* Robert Gambee, *Nantucket Island;* Kathryn Abbey Hanna, *Florida: Land of Change;* Francis Ross Holland, Jr., *America's Lighthouses;* Henry Beetle Hough, *Martha's Vineyard;* Katharine M. Jones, *Port Royal Under Six Flags;* Wallace Kaufman and Orrin Pilkey, *The Beaches Are Moving;* Robert Payne, *The Island;* David Beers Quinn (ed.), *The Roanoke Voyages 1584-1590*, Vols. I & II; Willie Lee Rose, *Rehearsal for Reconstruction;* Lyman V. Rutledge, *The Isles of Shoals, In Lore and Legend;* Chris Sherrill and Roger Aiello, *Key West: The Last Resort;* Dorothy Simpson, *The Maine Islands;* Edouard A. Stackpole, *The Sea Hunters;* David Stick, *The Outer Banks of North Carolina;* Arthur N. Strahler, *A Geologist's View of Cape Cod;* John and Mildred Teal, *Life and Death of a Salt Marsh;* Charlton W. Tebeau, *A History of Florida;* Bill Thomas, *The Island.*

Composition for *America's Atlantic Isles* by National Geographic's Photographic Services, Carl M. Shrader, Chief, Lawrence F. Ludwig, Assistant Chief. Printed and bound by Holladay-Tyler Printing Corp., Rockville, Md. Color separations by The Lanman Progressive Corp., Washington, D. C.; Lincoln Graphics, Inc., Cherry Hill, N.J.; N.E.C., Inc., Nashville, Tenn.